AGEING IN NORTH EAST INDIA
NAGALAND PERSPECTIVES

AGEING IN NORTH EAST INDIA

Nagaland Perspectives

Edited by

A. Lanunungsang Ao

AKANSHA PUBLISHING HOUSE
NEW DELHI (INDIA)

AKANSHA PUBLISHING HOUSE
4649-B/21, Ansari Road
Darya Ganj, New Delhi - 110 002
Email: ektabooks@yahoo.com
Ph. : 23263193 / 9811582579

Ageing in North East India: Nagaland Perspectives

First Published 2007

Reprint 2026

ISBN 978-81-8370-117-4

[The responsibility for the facts stated, conclusions reached etc. is entirely that of the Author. The publisher is not responsible for them, whatsoever.]

PRINTED IN INDIA

Published by Akansha Publishing House, New Delhi and Printed at Aryan Enterprises, Delhi.

FOREWORD

Ageing or becoming old is a global phenomenon in the sense that it is experienced by all the societies in all generations and all countries but its magnitude and manifestations are not the same everywhere. It has been observed that science and technology, industrialization, modernization and globalization like improved health care, improved nutrition and improved standards of living make people live much longer than expected and thereby there has been an increase in the growth of elderly population in all societies. The United Nations Principles for Older Persons in 1991 emphasized that *in all countries, individuals are reaching an advanced age in greater numbers and in better health than ever before.* The rise in the population of the elderly was thought to be a concern only of the developed countries but now it has become an equally important issue even in the developing countries as well. The population aged 60+ is increasing rapidly in our country that it is expected to be 177 million by 2025. This growth in the population of the elderly will certainly change the aspect of life for individual and societies.

It is a known fact that the old people in the past especially in our country commanded respect because they controlled the sources of power, wealth, land, political office, and the fate of other family members. However, it has been observed that there have been some changes in the society as new generations perceive a different outlook in life which are due to the pressures of urbanization, increasing migration from rural to urban areas, change in occupation patterns and perhaps a change in life styles too. Old age is also generally accompanied by a number of problems that the elderly have to face and adjust with in varying degrees. The problems of elderly are generally rooted in physical debility, loneliness and depression. Thus, their physical resources vary according to their age, lifestyle, genetic build and destiny. The important variables for the elderly are health and income. Therefore, the loss of economic independence and physical vigour and the emergence of various types of degenerative diseases, such as, hypertension, diabetes, rheumatism, gout, prostate, cardiac problems, spondylitis, lumbago, cancer, etc., often change an elderly from an independent self-supporting individual to one who needs help from his children, members of the family and the society in general. Absence of common interests and lack of extensive and regular interaction with the younger members in the family may result in social isolation and loneliness of the elderly.

There has been a time when the elders were kept in high esteem and phrases such as *old is gold; the older the wiser; country needs older people; you held our hands when we learnt to walk; now, as you enter the autumn of your lives, society is prepared to hold your hands*; etc., were appreciated much. While in some societies, the elders were neglected, left alone uncared when the children got married and separated. Whereas in other societies there were joint families where parents and married children lived together sharing everything together. However, this culture has now slowly broken in many conservative societies. Time and life has changed so fast due to science and technology and even the Gandhian philosophy of simple living and high thinking have become redundant in many families. With no income and incapable of working, many aged people become a burden on their children. Even if they are well looked-after, they suffer from a guilt complex. As a result, elders are neglected for some generations and suffer physically and mentally at the fag end of their life. In a befitting manner the former U.N Secretary General, Kofi Annan, in the Second World Assembly on Ageing in Madrid emphatically declared:

> "We have neglected the elders for many years. From now on, all the countries of the world should think to give proper to the senior citizens, in the last phase of their life, while making national development plans - social, political and economic."

It is heartening to note that, the UPA government is preparing a bill to improve the condition of the elderly persons in India. The bill that is on the anvil should certainly address the problems of the old people.

In the recent years, much literature on Northeast India has been published by the scholars of this region on various issues related to the people and the region as a whole. However, the issues related to ageing and the elderly persons of this region are not properly addressed so far. Although every 1st October is being observed as the International Day for the Elderly, yet the magnitude of the elderly persons in Northeast is not properly addressed neither in myriad seminars organised by various academic bodies and the NGOs nor their problems and aspirations are documented. Considering the lacunae in this field, the Indian Council of Social Science Research, North Eastern Regional Centre (ICSSR-NERC) took the initiative to bridge the gap by organizing a day long seminar on the **Magnitude of the Problems of the Elderly persons in** various States during the year 2006. This book has its origin in one of the seminars organized at the Department of Sociology, Nagaland University on 17th August 2006. Professor Lanu and his colleagues in the department took the keen interest in the seminar not only in organizing it but also compiling and revising the papers presented in the seminar in the present book format.

This book deals with a number of issues pertaining to the aged from a multi-disciplinary approach emphasizing on the status, welfare and problems of the elderly persons particularly in Nagaland and it will be a useful source of information and reference to academicians, scholars and social workers and government agencies alike.

Country Needs More Elderly Persons.

C JOSHUA THOMAS
Acting Director
ICSSR-NERC
Shillong

CONTENTS

LIST OF CONTRIBUTORS

Ao, Dr. Takatemjen, Principal, Clark Theological College, Aolijen.

Atsongchanger, Dr. Mar, Principal, Agape Bible College, Dimapur, Nagaland.

Baruah, D., Retd. OSD (Edu.).

Dzuvichu, Dr. Ketshukietuo, Principal, Oriental College, Kohima, Nagaland.

Gupta, Prof. S.K., Department of Education, Nagaland University, Kohima Campus, Kohima, Nagaland.

Jamir, Dr. I. Tongdangba, President, Pensioners' Association, Mokokchung District, Nagaland.

Lanunungsang, Prof. A., Department of Sociology, Nagaland University and Director, Centre for Gandhian Studies, Lumami Campus, Nagaland.

Lal, Prof. Pardeshi, Department of Zoology, Nagaland University, Lumami, Nagaland.

Medem, Dr. P., Medical Superintendent, Imkongliba Memorial Hospital, Mokokchung.

Singh, Dr. Chandrika, Department of Political Science, Nagland University, Lumami, Nagaland.

Visielie, Department of Sociology, Sazolie College, Kohima, Nagaland.

LIST OF TABLES

CHAPTER 3

CHAPTER 4

CHAPTER 5

INTRODUCTION

—A. Lanunungsang

As a biological factor, aging is a universal phenomenon. This is one of the most neglected areas in the society that needs due attention. It is a natural occurrence that may be experienced by one and all if not by every family. As a matter of fact, elderly people suffer from various problems such as health-care, shelter, nutrition, psychological problems, loneliness, family separation, non-availability of opportunities such as doctors, nurses, hospitals and nursing homes and negligence by the society etc. All these need proper understanding, due care and counselling. An aged person needs special care to overcome these problems; which can be attended not only by the government but also by non-governmental organizations, civil societies and individuals. In the past, this problem was not discussed in many forums though it is considered as one of the challenging areas of concern.

Many people may think that medical doctors and nurses are the only persons who can take care of the problems of the old aged persons but that is not enough. Today, medical practitioners and researchers are playing the most pivotal role; but apart from physical care, there are many concerns of the old aged persons in society. Therefore, in addition to medical practitioners, social workers, academic and religious organizations can also play a major role in caring for them in different ways. They should not be allowed to remain as the victims or unwanted creatures in the society. They need due recognition and understanding in the society beginning from the family circles, institution, governmental organization and voluntary organizations. They can provide constructive suggestions for the interest of such groups of people in the society. Their suggestions would be of great help for the policy and decision makers including the guardians of old aged persons in contemporary society.

One should not forget that elderly persons are the best advisors and consultants in every society and therefore, society needs them. They should not be treated as a liability in the family and society but considered as a social asset, dignity and the pride of a family and society at large.

Considering all these aspects, we have chosen a common theme as ***Understanding the Problems of Old and Aged People and the Need for Care.***

Under this theme, many areas of interest were deliberated in a day long seminar held on 17 August 2006 at the Department of Sociology, Nagaland University covering wide areas such as biological aspects, health, psychological, socio-economic concerns, management and organizational aspects, institutions and policy matters, administration welfare schemes and social planning aspects etc. To be more specific, following sub-themes were discussed:

- Identification of various problems faced by old aged persons such as basic needs of life, (shelter, health, food, physiological etc.), extent of negligence by the society and family.
- Management aspects of old aged persons and role of family, relatives, institutions, churches, NGOs, civil societies, governmental organizations, hospitals and nursing homes etc.

- Old age and pensioners syndrome, retired life and their limitations and social response,
- Potentialities and capacity, leadership, status and roles, vision and their contributions in the society,
- Social concerns for old aged persons, victims of the society and the need for proper understanding and care,
- Assessment of their contributions in society and peoples' and governments response, failures and success,
- Customary relations to old aged persons, cultural practices. family norms and the extent of care for old aged persons,
- Gender role, gender bias, sexual dichotomy of gender role towards old aged persons in Naga society,
- Anthro-biological aspects of old aged persons, aging problems and trend, assessment or grave-yards, longevity, climatic and environmental effect and joy of rejuvenation and challenges of old aged persons,
- The need for establishment of Old Aged Home, people support and prospects and scope in Naga society,
- The Naga Pensioners' Association, their roles performance, difficulties of drawing pension, difficulties faced in Accountant General Office, Treasury, Bank and governmental departments and remedial measures for change.
- Rural-urban dichotomy of old aged persons, status, push and pull factors of migration, issues for burial, customary relation and its implication in Naga society,

- Socio-economic status of old aged persons and the need for proper care, acceptance and rejection of the ideas/voices of the elderly people and generation gap,
- Parental, social, governmental, institutional, NGOs and religious institutional care for elderly people in Naga society,
- Christian concerns and the role of church in caring and counseling, social and spiritual backup, entertainment programs and preparation of their last journey for happy life ending.
- Social laws, payment of old age pension; its awareness and welfare schemes for old age persons, difficulties and solutions,
- Suggestive measures for proper management and care for those section of people and the need for total salvation (body, mind and soul), the need for physical care.

This book is an outcome of the above-mentioned seminar jointly sponsored by the Indian Council of Social Science Research, North Eastern Regional Centre (ICSSR-NERC), Shillong and Centre for Gandhian Studies and Research, Nagaland University. It contains nine papers presented during the seminar. The authors of these articles are mostly teachers of the Nagaland University and its affiliated colleges. Few of them are activists working among the elderly people of Nagaland. We are pleased to present the revised papers presented in the seminar for wider deliberation.

We acknowledge with thanks for the financial assistance and the motivating force which the ICSSR-NERC extended towards this seminar. We also thankfully acknowledge the Centre for Gandhian Studies and Research, Nagaland University for granting additional fund for the success of this seminar. We particularly put on record our thanks and appreciation to Dr. C. Joshua Thomas, Director, ICSSR-NERC for the driving force behind this seminar. But for his constant reminders and encouragement this volume would not have seen its light.

How can Society Neglect the Elderly People?

KEYNOTE ADDRESS

—Dr. Takatemjen Ao

All over the world there is an increase in the population of old people. This revolution of longevity has made many communities to gear up for meeting the challenge, as it will be the first time in the history of the world that the number of sixty plus (60+) people will outnumber the under 15 category.

The National Policy on Older Persons (NPOP) acknowledges the fact that in the coming decades a growing number of persons 60+ will belong to the middle and upper middle-income groups. It is highly probable that they will reside in urban areas. The social and economic factors that impact the lives of present day senior citizens in urban areas are:

Better health care and advances in the field of medicine, people live healthy into their old age. Even the elderly with ailments live better lives;

Many people lead active lives into their 60's and even 70's, but retirement continues to be at 58 or 60;

More and more youngsters seeks their fortunes in other countries and as a result many elderly couples live on their own;

"Small family" norm sees just one or two children having to share the responsibility of their parents.

When we talk about the Old people we need to be sensitive not to classify all the elderly under one category of 'old'. After all, with people living well into their mid eighties, the elderly cover a whole generation of people! The National Policy for Old People refers to them as 'young old' (between 60-69 years) middle old (70-79) and the 'Older Old' (80 and above). Hence the community of senior citizens should not be looked upon only as 'demanding attention' but be seen as a resource base too. Also, the services for older people can be very varied, from health care to recreation.

Growth Trend in Population of Elderly in India (>60 Years)

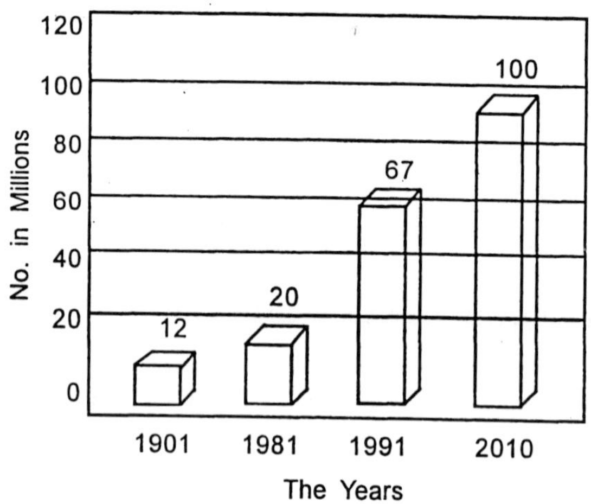

In 1991, there were about 67 million older people in India and is expected to go up to 100 million by 2016. This is a grim picture, which every state or the Government of India is going to face. In 1999, to commemorate the year of older persons, the Government of India had announced a National Policy on Older

Persons and consitituted a National Council on Ageing. The outcome of these initiatives is awaited. No doubt, the government has many other issues of concern and the action plan is eagerly awaited.

We have a long way to go before the issue gains visibility it warrants. There is no escape from age, and no escape from the issue that face the society, a country and a people. Unfortunately, both the Constitution and laws so far as India is concerned, have made noble and progressive commitments that sound very good on paper but in practice there is very little done. The policy on older persons has indications of progress, it has good things, but in the magnitude of the problem it is miserably inadequate, because it does not address either the magnitude of the challenge or the quality of the challenge.

Some issues which a seminar like today can take up for deliberation are:

1. Problems faced by elderly people and their needs and the response of societies.
2. The role of the Government, NGO's and the church in taking care of elderly people.
3. Traditional societies and elderly people.
4. The need for the establishment of old aged homes in our societies.
5. Management of old aged persons.
6. The pensioners' association, the pensioners' problems, etc.
7. Pastoral care and counselling of the elderly persons from a Christian perspective.
8. Rural-urban dichotomy of elderly people and its implications.

9. Utilising the services of the elderly people: Their potentialities and roles in society.
10. Successful Aging.

As a theological educator, here I would like to present a few important thoughts regarding the problem of the elderly people of our land from a theological perspective.

Understanding the Problems and the Process of Aging: A Theological Perspective

Human development is the process of change and growth—psychologically, biologically, socially and spiritually. The most common identified life stages are infancy, childhood, adolescence, adulthood, middle age and old age. Studies on human growth and development provide a good understanding of the nature and the needs of individuals at all developmental levels. Old age denotes the gradual decay of human physical system which becomes more remarkable towards the end of life, ending in the breaking of the system and so death. Elderly people have their own peculiar characteristics, problems and needs where successful aging becomes one of its issues.

Some needs of Elderly People are:

1. Adapting to a revised physical self-image.
2. The need for the integration of various losses (loss of health, loss of identity, loss of power, loss of independence, loss of spouse, loss in the level of incomes).
3. The feeling of continuing usefulness.
4. The need for love, care, involvement and companionship.
5. The need for meeting spiritual needs. They need spiritual support. The need for finding meaning in life and affirmation of onself.

Successful Aging

One cannot stop growing old, but one can grow old gracefully. There are two criteria for judging successful aging. The first is the satisfaction the elderly people have in them and the other is the social role and interpersonal obligations and responsibility. Implied in the concept of successful aging is the value judgement to the effect that some adjustments are better (successful) than some (unsuccessful). If one were to age successfully, it would mean successfully coping with disengagement. The age successfully the individual should avoid shrinkage of life space and find substitute when necessary. In terms of personality, people are said to have aged successfully if they maintain a matured and integrated personality while going through the aging process. The life satisfaction approach holds that people have aged successfully if they feel happy and satisfied with their present and past lives. Successful aging is defined both as autonomous and persistent. If the overall relation of the individual to the society system is both autonomous and persistent, the person is aging successfully.

Hochschild identified six general themes that constitute a basis for successful aging: (1) sufficient independence to allow continued feelings of integrity; (2) pleasant, satisfying relationships with other people, some of whom are willing to provide assistance when needed, without in the process showing a disrespect for older persons; (3) a reasonable degree of emotional and physical satisfaction and a comfortable physical environment; (4) stimulation of the mind in ways that are not too strenuous; (5) sufficient mobility to be able to experience varied environments; and (6) some type of intense life interest or involvement, at least partly to avoid preoccupation with thoughts of death.

Care for the Elderly: A Holistic Approach

Respect and care is deeply rooted in Jewish tradition. The Old Testament talks about "honouring father and mother" (Exo 20:12; Lev 19:32). Honouring implies caring for them in their old age (Gen 45:9-11, Ecc 3:12). In particular, care is to be given to those whose parents are feebleminded.

Help and care towards the elderly persons demands a wholistic approach that will provide them the opportunity to enjoy life to its fullest. From the point of view of care and counselling bringing wholeness to an older person involves six dimensions, namely, enlivening one's mind, revitalizing one's body, renewing and enriching one's intimate relationships, deepening one's relationship with nature and biosphere, growth in relation to the significant institutions in one's life, deepening and revitalizing one's relationship with God.

Growth in humans takes place in relationships, six of which are listed above. Growth towards wholeness in one dimension stimulates and support in the other dimension. Holistic care and counselling aim at enabling process to increase and balance growth in all aspects of their lives. Mental-spiritual health is the continuing movement towards living more fully, joyfully and productively. Therefore, facilitating the six dimensions of holistic care and counselling of the elderly should be emphasized to let the elderly experience wholeness of life.

The U.N. principles for older persons also reflect this approach:

1. *Principle of Independence* - Older persons have access to food, water, shelter, clothing, healthcare and income-generating opportunities, education, and training.

2. *Principle of Care* - Older persons should have access to social and legal service and to healthcare so that they can maintain an optimum level of physical, mental, emotional well-being. These should include full respect for dignity, beliefs, needs and privacy.

3. *Principle of Self-fulfilment* - Older persons should have access to educational, cultural, educational and recreational resources and be able to develop their full potentiality.

4. *Principle of Participation* - Older persons should remain integrated into community life and participate actively in the formation of policies affecting their well-being.

5. *Principle of Dignity* - Older persons should be able to live in dignity and security, be free from exploitation and physical and mental abuse and be treated fairly regardless of age, gender, racial and ethnic background.

Theological Response to Successful Aging

1. Aging is a process of growth and fulfilment. From a developmental point of view and from theological understanding, aging should be seen as "growing", "coming of age", "getting on in years". Though aging is a time of decline, there is growth in the process. The body is wasting away, but the inner person is renewed everyday. And therefore, there is fulfilment in aging.

2. Aging is a process of finding meaning in life. People need sound values and meaning to be healthy. Finding meaning in life is also an important concern for the aged, through life review and reminiscense, a sense of wholeness can be achieved. Life review may bring repentance, forgiveness and acceptance which

are the key theological components of integrity. It may also give new and significant meanings to one's life and also prepare one for death.

3. Aging is an affirmation of one's life's worth. The aging process involves the questions of living, dying and suffering, which is based on an important theological or spiritual issue. Is life woth living? In other words, the main developmental or spiritual task, which the aging process demands is that of developing a sense of life's worth. The deciding factor of whether or not the experience of loss in old age can be used meaningfully for his or her benefit is the attitude of the individual's faith and one's perception of life.

Old is Gold

REFERENCES

1. Hochschild, A.R., *The Unexpected Community*, New Jersey: Prentice-Hall Inc., 1973.
2. Kumar, Vilasiri and Jayanthi Nayak, "Nightingales Elders Environment Centre: A Profile". From the Internet.
3. Radhakrishnan, G.N. Sunanda, "The Aging Issue and Community Participation". From the Internet.
4. Rogers, Dorothy, *The Adult Years: An Introduction to Aging*, New Jersey: Prentice-Hall, Inc., 1979.

1

PROBLEM OF OLD-AGE PEOPLE AND SOCIAL REMEDY

—Chandrika Singh

Aging is a natural as well as incessant process, which begins with birth and ends with death. In this modern world no one can escape the flow of birth and death. One, who comes into existence or is born, is bound to die one day. The life is a constant journey, which passes through various mile stones. The destiny of each living being is to grow older and older and one day disappears from the existence. Oldness is the last stage of journey of the life where one has to face various kinds of troubles. Hence, no one likes to be old and suffer, but there is no way to escape, from it. It is bound to come. Hence, one must be mentally ready to meet it and physically fit to face it. Mahatma Gandhi used to say that *death is our best friend which gives us permanent rest.* We should meet death as a friend because it permanently relieves us from bondage of the world. Death comes without any hint or information while oldness reaches knocking the door. Death relieves one from the responsibilities of the life forever while oldness releases one from botheration of active life. Since it is impossible to escape old age and death, it is wise to be ever ready to embrace both death and oldness when they come to us. Death and oldness both are reality of the life. Hence, it is better to be ready to welcome the reality with big strength and large heart.

No doubt, the stage of oldness has numerous problems, but there are remedies too to meet the challenges of old age. There are ways to help the aged people to live comfortably and satisfactorily. The responsibility of the family and society to look after its old people is greater. The old people have to live in the society and society may evolve certain measures to assist them. Old people cannot be taken as liabilities. Though they cannot work hard and earn, but their long experience of the life is great asset not only for the family members but for the society as a whole. The responsibility of the old people does not end with growing old. An old adage says, old is gold. Old people cannot be treated useless or worthless heap. Even during old age they may play many roles in the interest of the society.

This paper discusses about meaning of the old age and its problems. It talks about the responsibility of society towards old people and suggests some remedial measures to help the old people. It also analyses and evaluates the role of the government towards old people.

Man and Society

Man and society has perpetual and reciprocal relationship. It is universal and undisputable fact that man is a social animal by nature. Man is born in society, lives and prospers in society and ultimately he takes his last breathe in society. Society is in the nature and blood of the man. Both depend upon each other. Society helps man in each and every walk of life by creating favourable circumstances to live without fear and prosper according to the choice while man contributes a lot to society by working hard, generating new ideas, creating new science, technology, arts, literature etc.

Neither man can live without society nor can society prosper without man's contributions. Aristotle, the great ancient Greek philosopher, has rightly said that those who live without a society is either a beast or a god.

Human society is an organised and civilized way of living. A society is comprised of different types of people who differ in their way of living, but they are bound to live together supporting each other. Every one has assigned role to perform responsibilities in the greater interest of society as a whole. When we talk of civil society, it means, a society which is civilized and where there is no room for barbarism and arbitrary behaviour. It is society, which teaches man how to live and how to behave. A society cannot be called civilized where its members are not permitted to live freely and follow the course of life which is beneficial not only to him but to the society at large.

Society comprises of families, clans, castes, various social groups, such as religious, economic, cultural, and ethical. Numerous non-governmental groups or institutions are allowed to emerge in a society and act in the interest their members. Society does not permit to grow evils and anti-social elements. If such evils or elements are there, the society takes up the steps to curb them or to eradicate them for ever. Hence society has certain norms to punish the people who do not abide by the social norms or who harm the social interests.

Again, society is prior to state and government both. The state and government came into existence with the marked objectives to protect people, create favourable circumstance for better life and pave the way for further growth of healthy society. They also play the role to help those who need social security and assistance. Society has numerous social norms, customs, usages, traditions, cultures, behaviours, practices, bindings, etc., which evolved from the time immemorial with the objectives to keep the society intact and maintain the social relations without harming anyone. Social bindings are there, but for correction, not for destruction. Society has place and provision for every one right from his birth to death. Society is so big and great that it has norms and rituals for its members who are no more in the world.

Every one is the member of society. Society has to take care of all its members whether they are young or old, weak or strong, educated or uneducated and rich or poor. In a civilized society there are different layers of the groups of the people according to their origin, faith, religion, economic status, and social up gradation. The beauty of a good society is that, everyone occupies honourable place according to his/her understanding. Each group is allowed to prosper without harming each other. Family is the basic unit of the society. It is the family that takes care of and supports its members right from the birth to death. It is the family, which is the base of development of its members. The family is the tie based on blood relationship having mutual affection and love for each other. The family has to share both the liabilities and assets of its members. The second grade of society is the clan, tribe and caste. According to Hegel, the western social and political philosopher, what we talk of tribe or caste is the developed form of the family only. That is why it is based on racial as well as blood relationship. Hence, it is the bounded duty of the family to take care of its old members and solve the problems of old-aged persons.

Meaning of Old Age

Old age cannot be defined exactly because it does not have the same meaning in all societies. In many parts of the world, people are considered old because of certain changes in their activities and physical appearance. Old people have limited regenerative abilities and more prone to disease, syndromes and sickness than other adults. Again, people may be considered old when they become grandparents or when they begin to do less or different work. Moreover, the old people belong to an unproductive minority, and their fate depends upon the interests of the active majority.

Hence, it is difficult to give a precise definition of old-age and determine the exact period or time from where one lands into the arena of old-age. The citizens above the age of sixty five years are generally designated as the senior citizen. The age of superannuation, may also be called as the old-age. However, the age of superannuation differs from the range of 57 to even 70 years. The perception behind superannuation is that the incumbent's physical strength is not able to sustain the labour, which is required. Generally the sensual as well as physical organs of the old people are not as effective as they were during the period of youth.

In the United States, people are often considered old if they have lived a certain number of years. Many Americans think 65 is the beginning of old age because Unites States workers become eligible to return with full social security benefits at the age of 65. People in the 65-over age group are often called "senior citizens".

Worldwide, the number of people 65-year old or above is increasing faster than ever before in the developing countries because of better facilities of medication. In the US the percentage of people 65 or older increased from 4% in 1990 to about 13% in the last 1990s. In 1990, only about 3 million of the nation's population had reached 65. By 1998, the number of senior citizens had increased to about 34 million. The number of elderly people is growing around the world chiefly because more children reach adulthood. In most parts of the world, women live, on average, longer than men. In the U.S. in the late 1990s, life expectancy at birth was 80 years for women and 73 years for men. American women who were aged 65 in the late 1990s could expect to live about 19 additional years. Men who were 65 could expect to live about 19 additional years.

India, like many other developing countries in the world, is presently witnessing rapid ageing of its population. Almost eight out of ten older people in India live in rural areas. Urbanization, modernization and globalization have led to changes in economic structure, erosion of societal values and the weakening of social institutions such as the joint family. In this changing economic and social milieu, the younger generation is too much busy in searching new identities where they can enjoy economic independence and adjust with the fast changing society. The changing economic structure has reduced the dependence of rural families on land, which had provided strength to bonds between generations. The traditional sense of duty and obligation of the younger generation towards their older generation is being eroded. The older generation is caught between the decline in traditional values on the one hand and the absence of an adequate social security system on the other.

Any way, the problem of the old-aged people is their well-being. Old people have to depend upon other for their well-being and survival because they are physically weak and their vital organs like eyes, ears, hands, legs, lungs, heart etc. are not in position to work effectively. Old people, in fact, have to depend on others in many ways. They may fall victims to various kinds of diseases frequently, where they need physical service as well as immediate and proper care and treatment. The body of the old person becomes the home of diseases because it can hardly sustain the bacterial and viral attacks. Some one has rightly said that oldness is a disease in itself. Or old-age body is the home of diseases. They have to depend upon others for proper care and nursing. If they are not looked after properly, they may have to face numerous troubles and inconveniences.

Problem of the Old People and Certain Remedies

The memory power of the old people goes down and it becomes difficult for them to remember the past events or even to recognize the people whom they were well acquainted. At this situation they feel embarrassment. The vision of the eyes weakens due to cataract or other kind of eye diseases. If proper attention is not paid in time, they may be blind, which may add further troubles to them. In absence of timely and proper care they may be the victim of paralysis or other neurological problems, which add more troubles to the family. Constant period of depression may result in madness also. Thus, old age is such a stage of mankind where the old people need special care, assistance, well behaviour, hospitability, medical treatment and social attachment.

One of the greatest universal problems of the old people is lacking family as well as social attachment. The body becomes old, no doubt, but feelings, sentiments, emotions, wishes and desires of the old people never die. Hence, they need family as well as social attachments. It has generally been observed that old people are deprived of social attachments because hardly one has time to share emotional and sentimental feeling with the old people. It is all because, today, when life has become so busy, tough and hard, everyone is busy for self development and economic prosperity. Even the family members have no much time to spare for their retired elders. As a result, the old person feels himself/herself partially or totally neglected that ultimately results in the state of melancholy and depression. Hence, an old person needs psychological attachment from the family members and honours as well as regard from the society. He/she requires companionship to get rid of melancholy and loneliness.

He/she wants to get rid of perpetual monotony, dullness, boredom etc. Work keeps man busy and it is easy for him to pass the time, but old people without work become bore and it is much difficult for them to pass time. They feel lonely.

It should not be forgotten that when the old people were young and strong, they commanded respect and honour in both the family and society. In fact, the old man/woman is the root of the family tree and pioneer of the society. Before coming to the period of old-age, each guardian of the family concerned happened to be the leader of the house. It is he/she who used to take care of the children, arrange their better education, earn wealth for the support and survival of the family members and take trouble to provide them comforts. No family could prosper unless the guardian would have sacrificed for the prosperity of the family. At the same time, the old people had the opportunities to contribute a lot for the growth of society. When they were young, they played various roles to lead the society towards betterment by working hard in the fields, offices, factories, industries and serving border areas as a soldier. Their contributions to upgrade society by fighting with anti-social elements, helping the social organizations and contributing valuable suggestions cannot be overlooked. While working as brave soldiers, good public leaders, committed bureaucrats, village leaders, members of various social organizations, farmers, workers, poets, authors, dramatists, novelists etc, the old people did a lot to increase the name and fame of the society as well as the nation. Such old persons expect at least respect and regard from the members of the family, society and the government of the nation.

Hence, the family, the society and the nation have to acknowledge contributions of the old people and pay back them prices for their good services what they did to the family, the society and the nation at the stage when they are old. No society, which claims to be good, may turn deaf ears or blind eyes to the needs of the old people. No grown up members of the family should be blind to the requirements of their old and retired members. They have to pay back their debt to their elders. No nation, which is well advanced, may boycott the old people. The old people are not liabilities of the family, society or the nation only because they are too old to work. They must be taken as assets. Hence, it is the responsibility of the civilized society to ensure that the old people are not neglected and abandoned.

Majority of the old people in developing or under-developed countries are uninsured by formal social security programmes. The most traditional system is the family support, which still has a supplementary role to play. Some countries like Netherlands, Denmark, Norway, Canada, New Zealand and Australia do not have problems of 'uninsured old' because they have universal flat (uniform) or very broad means-tested old-age security benefits. In these countries the old-age benefits is typically financed out of general revenues and all residents are eligible to receive the benefits at old age. Once the people reach the specified age, the care is taken either by the government or by the non-governmental institutions (NGOs). Here, the problem is to manage the proper finance. System is that, the advanced people are kind enough to pay taxes to meet the expenditure on the needs of the old-age people. Another way to solve the problem of finance is volunteer contribution to extend pension insurance to those who do not have covered pensionable jobs. In Japan, men are encouraged to make contributions for their wives. In China, workers are pressurized to contribute to their individual accounts on a volunteer basis. But here, problem is the low payment of the workers. In India, field workers' payment is too low to save even a little amount for their future security.

Moreover, the majority of the workers who are illiterate hardly understand the significance of savings.

Old-Age People whether Assets or Liabilities of the Family?

Each old person has his/her home and family. Each family has moral as well legal responsibility to see and look after its old members. A general survey of the conditions of old people in India either in the rural or urban areas envisages the truth that the majority of the old people are not happy and satisfied. So long as the old members of the family are in a position to earn, the family takes care of them, but when they are unable or physically unfit to work and earn, the family generally takes such members as liabilities. There are few families, which have proper care and give respect and honour to their old people. Specially among the poor families the conditions of the old people are very much deplorable. Poverty of such families are main hurdles before them to have proper care for their old people. They can provide them neither nutritious food nor proper medical treatment. As a result, several of the old persons not only face the hardships of the life but also die before time. The behaviours of members of such poor families towards the old people have been found rough and tough perhaps due to economic frustration or lack of good family culture. There are numerous old people in India who are half-fed and half-clothed. There is no medical treatment for them. That is why several of them die before time in absence of better care and treatment. They are the victims of economic crisis. There is no old age home where they can pass their time. There is no one who can share their problems and shed tears for them. They are left on their own fate that is the fate of sufferings.

The problem of the retired or old age persons of the middle class and rich family is not economic crisis, but lack of concern to their elders. Every adult member is too busy to spare time and share their problems. No doubt, the old persons of such family are lucky enough to get their economic problems solved, but what they lack is proper company of the family members. Even after they return back from the service, they are found busy with certain affairs. They are found participating in night clubs, picture halls and, visiting friends' houses till late night. Moreover, they watch various programmes on television, while the old people are left alone or at the mercy of the servants who can hardly give them emotional family touch.

It does not mean that Indian families or society do not take care of the retired family members. Relationship of family members in India is based on religious base. India is virtually a religious country. It may be Hinduism, Christianity, Islamism or Sikhism, all religions teach the followers to respect elders and serve them more when they become old. India believes in blessing of elders. Each society in India has honourable place for elders. It is the bounded duty of the sons and daughters to take care of their old and retired parents and meet the cost of their requirements. That is why the conditions of the Indian old people in comparison to that of the other nations of the world, is far better. They are not allowed to suffer and die without care. Even after death the family members of the diseased perform certain rituals with the marked objective to provide peace and salvation to the departed souls. However, problem is that in an advanced and industrialized society where consumerism has come on forefront, no one has time to look after their old people. In absence of proper jobs and professions many families are frustrated today. In such a situation, the religious sermons hardly help them to be true to their duties.

Thus, the problems before most of the Indian families for looking after their old people are mass poverty, economic crisis, uncertainty of future etc. They have no money to give proper medical treatment to their members. They have no sufficient facilities to share with their people. They have to work hard living behind their old people because it is the compulsion. Most of the families in India are hand to mouth. Even survival is a big problem for these poor and deprived sections of people. Hence, they can neither think of taking proper care nor give better treatment to their old or retired people.

Government's Efforts to Assist Old People

General observation of the government's steps taken towards providing relief to the old people in India reveals the fact that nothing effectively has been done so far in this regard. Welfarism and altruism, which has become the basic base of governance of the modern government, have brought into force various programmes for the well-being of people under the caption social security. Social security is a general term, which has various devices to help the needy people. But most of the schemes under social security are related to the government servants. Under such provisions the government servants are provided with the facilities such as quarters or house rent, benefit of GPF, medical treatment, allowance for children education, increased dearness and pension facility. Thus, the benefits under the social securities mostly go to the government servants. The pension and retirement benefits which they get after retirement are enough to maintain their life peacefully. They have no worry to suffer economically.

So far the case of the general old people is concerned, nothing notable step has been taken so far. It is true that the government has launched certain schemes to give economic relief to the senior citizens. There is provision to give them more interest on their money invested or deposited in the banks and some rebate in income tax, too. They are also given more interest benefits on various money deposit schemes in the banks and post offices etc. These all help the retired government servants to lead self-dependent life. So far the case of the unemployed old people is concerned, there is no provision at all to provide them economic relief except the old-age pension to some selected people belonging to the sections of the poor, suppressed, neglected and downtrodden. Major shortcoming of such scheme is that the amount, which is given in the name of old age pension, is too little to meet even daily minimum requirement of the life. Moreover, the scheme does not cover even 10% of the people who are old and in dire need of economic assistance. As a result, major portion of the old people of India specially in the rural areas are unlooked and uncared for. They have to solely rely upon the care of the family members. No doubt, the government of India has recently opened certain schemes of welfare for the old people such as concession in traveling, postal saving scheme, etc., but it may hardly help the poor old people to get relief. Until the Government opens major scheme for the welfare of the old people, their problems are not going to be over.

Except in few metropolitan cities in India there is no Old-Age Care Home. There is no public place where the old people can get together and pass their time while playing some sorts of game or reading news papers and magazines. In Kerala and Madras, there are few Old-Age Care Homes where the old people are admitted and properly looked after. Though the people living in these Homes are deprived of family love and affection, they have been found happy only because they have sufficient means to pass time and share feeling with their fellow friends. Moreover, their needs are properly met and they avail timely medical treatment also. They have the freedom to go home and meet their family members. The family members, too, attend the Care

Home from time to time to see whether their people are well or not. Such practice should be extended to other parts of the country. But it is notable that such facilities can be availed by the family which is rich enough to afford the required expenditure. Here, the government may play vital role to set up and maintain such Homes. The old members of the poor family may be given some sort of stipend or monetary assistance to meet the expenditure.

Role of the Family and Society towards the Old People

To help and assist the old people there is an immediate need to change attitude towards the old people. We cannot take them as burden. There are many families where the old people are badly treated and cursed upon. We must not forget that the old people are the gems of the society. They are the vast treasury of experience and knowledge. They are the root of the family and the society. They are fathers, mothers, grand-fathers and grand-mothers. They are the well-wishers of the family and society. They expect good behaviour and favourable response from the family and society. They have the maturity to guide young towards the way of prosperity and happiness. They know what is good and what is bad. They carry with themselves experienced and tested knowledge of life. They have seen many ups in their life and come crossed them successfully. They know how to live happily and how to behave properly. They have the wisdom to guide their family members especially during the period of crisis.

Thus, keeping in view the facts mentioned above the society must take the benefits of old people's experience and knowledge. The society must accord respect and honour for the old because they deserve that. The attitude of the society towards the old people should be sympathetic and cooperative. It may be social or family functions, the old people should be invited generously. They should be given hounarable place in such functions and they should be invited to share their views and opinions on such occasions. If possible they should be publicly awarded for the deeds what they had done for the society and the nation. During the time of crisis the society must come ahead to assist and help the old people even through money contributions. The young people should behave respectfully with the old persons. Their problems should be duly considered and satisfactorily taken into account.

In India, blessing of the old has high place in the society. It is believed that their blessing brings prosperity and happiness in the life of the blessed one. Hence, all the efforts should be applied to win over them and obtain their good blessings. Even a word of love and sympathy may win over the heart of the old people because they are mild and simple. It is the bounden responsibility of the family members to have constant care for their old people and serve them as per their needs. They can help them by cleaning their cloth, washing their body, giving them timely food, nursing them during sickness and keeping them happy. They should be provided with certain kinds of amusements. If the old people are educated, they should be provided with newspapers, journals, magazines etc. to pass time and be update about happenings of the world.

Responsibility of the Old People towards Themselves

It has generally been observed that many old people are the victim of psychological thinking. They view oldness as burden upon themselves and even upon the family. This is negative attitude, which brings them near disappointment, frustration and worries. The oldness is the common problem for every one. Oldness is not a curse, but a boon. Those who die before being old are unlucky and unfortunate. God has given life to live with determination and hope. Strong and positive mental attitude helps every one either young or old to live happily. The old people must not think that they are neglected lot and worthless fellows. Rather, they should be proud of their contributions which they had done for the rise and growth of their families and development of the society. They should not take themselves as the burden on the family or society. Rather, they should think that they are experienced people and society needs their valuable suggestions because old is gold.

There are many ways, which can help them in maintaining their health and live happily. The old people must be aware of their daily routine and control their diets. They must keep themselves away from injurious habits such as drinking, smoking, chewing *pans* or *tamuls* and tobacco etc. They must adopt certain good habits, which give strength and protect one from diseases. It is said that the walking is the best exercise. Since the old people cannot do heavy exercise, they must develop the habit to do morning and evening exercise daily. If possible, they must do Yoga according to their capacity. By doing regular Yoga they can get rid of various diseases such as asthma (breathing problem), frequent attack of cough and cold, indigestion, gastric, constipation, problem of nervous system, heart and lungs trouble, insomnia etc. Concentration of the mind is a must to get mental peace. Hence, the old people should develop the habit of concentration of mind through Yoga.

Since the old people have enough time, they must attend prayer assembly everyday. Unbreakable faith in Almighty and His compassion and grace gives one mental peace and physical strength to live happily. The old people must devote their time to worship and pray to God. So far their attitude towards the family members and the society is concerned; the old people must not curse them. The family has numerous problems to be solved. The old members of the family should not add trouble to these problems. They must be cooperative, accommodative and helpful. They must have patience and endurance to tolerate inconveniences during the time of emergency. Their love and sympathy towards their family members should not be lessened. Their tune of talk with the people must be lovely and attractive. They should not be critics unnecessarily. Rather, they should have positive attitude for their people and appreciate their performances. Each generation has its own way of living and thinking. Hence, they should learn adjustment with new generation. They should be ready to make compromise with the ideas and feeling of new generation provided these are helpful and meaningful. The old people must not be disappointed. They must be hopeful about future. Thinking that nothing is permanent in this universe, they should live with hope and patience. They must have courage and be brave to face the challenges before them. They must not forget the "power of living" through "will power".

Conclusion

Thus, it is very much obvious that the problem of old-age in India is acute. In a fast changing industrial society where money power is playing vital role to adjust in society, the problems of the old people are multiplying day by day. With increasing number of workers the employees are asked to retire as early as possible so that the unemployed youths can avail the opportunity of employment. No doubt, the strength of the life of old people has increased, but the support of their life has decreased. Ernest Burgees, in *Aging in Western Societies* (1960) came to the conclusion that urbanization and the mass production of commodities are the chief which have undermined the economic basis of the extended family number of self-employed. This loss of extended family the aged and with their loss of decision-making power in the work arises pressures for their retirement.

Andurs Gerontology Centre, University of California, made a study on more traditional 'Free Homes' for the aged poor who have no family to care for them and the more recent for 'Pay Homes' for the middle-class. They also investigated a small number of 'Day-Care Centres'. According to the study, the most homes house which has small numbers of residents, have common spaces for dining, TV and prayer. The residents have access to medical care and transportation. They are provided meals and some assistance with activities of daily living. These centers are open to all castes. All are run by non-governmental organizations (NGOs), only one-third with government assistance. Free homes tend to be bigger and older, serve non-aged clients, have less privacy and emphasize occupational therapy and income-generating activities, and are more like board-and-care homes. For pay homes have more privacy and western-style amenities, focus on local community outreach and provide fewer meals.

The gradual increase of all old-age homes has given rise to debates about their appropriate roles in Indian society and about their quality. Government grants to NGOs for homes and day-care centers (often considered more appropriate support for elders) are limited. With the National Policy on Older Persons looking to NGOs and village councils to be the primary sources of non-familial aged care, several ways to build their capacity are suggested. Such practices must be increased in the Indian society to solve the problem, related to the old-age people. The government and NGOs' must come ahead with generosity to facilitate such day-care centers, Old Age Care Home etc. and increase their number so that good number of old-age people may be well accommodated.

We Respect Every Elderly Person

2

CONSTITUTIONAL PROVISIONS, PRIVILEGES AND BENEFITS TO OLD AGED PEOPLE

—S.K. Gupta

Life expectancy in India has improved over the last few decades. The number of 60+ persons which was 20 million in 1961 had increased to 56.7 million in 1991. The projected number in 2001 and 2016 is 76 and 113 million respectively which constitute 7.7% and 8.9% of total population. This is indicative of the increasing number of elderly people. This huge reserve of human resource needs to be productively utilized and their life long experience taken advantage for the benefit of the society.

The society is witnessing a gradual but definite withering of the joint family system as a result of which the elders in the family are exposed to emotional neglect and lack of physical and financial support. This has led to a situation where young are increasingly unable or unwilling to have parents living with them. This trend reveals that ageing will become a major social challenge in the future and vast resources will be required towards support, care and treatment of the older people. There is an emerging need to pay greater attention to ageing people and related issues to promote policies and programs for dealing with a future ageing. It was in this context that Ministry of Social Justice and Empowerment, Government of India announced a National Policy for Older Persons in Jan. 1999.

The policy provides a broad framework for inter-sectoral collaboration and cooperation both within the government as well as between government and non-government agencies. In particular, the policy has identified a number of areas of information, financial security, health care and nutrition, physical, mental and emotional, shelter, education, protection and life property etc. for the welfare of older persons in the country. The policy also provides active and productive involvement of older persons to utilize their experience arid services and not just their care.

Basing on a resource study on senior citizens in Nagaland, the major, findings and recommendations are as follows:

1. More than 60% of the elderly persons retired both from the government and private sectors were physically and mentally fit and expressed their willingness for re-employment
2. Only 11% of the elderly citizens were re-employed and happy with the work engaged after retirement. Most of these people are in need of re-employment due to financial constraints. It was recommended in the study report that qualified and skilled ones may be involved in administrative, consultative and developmental activities as per their expertise and experience.
3. 35% of the elderly persons suffer from various health problems like blood pressure, diabetes, cardiac and knee-joints etc. Many of them do not get medical facilities for their treatment. They expect financial help either from the government or society, as 70% of them stated that they do

not have adequate savings to meet their needs in old age.

Regarding the problems faced by elderly people in Nagaland, it was found that the old aged people lack:

I. Respect from the younger generation.

II. Recreational and medical facilities.

III. Funds to meet their day to day needs. The elderly people were also found ridden with tension and their concern to involvement of younger generation in anti-social activities and bad habits, HIV/AIDS menace and extortions etc.

Some of these people also face problem of isolation within the family and in the society. Most of them complained of physical sickness/and general weakness and no adequate effort either from the government or from the society to look after them. Many of them are not getting old age pension and other benefits due to them because of financial constraints in the state government. There are also lack of old age homes for meetings and share among themselves and spend leisure time. There is no provision for financial help provided to them if they wish to involve themselves in self-employed schemes along with their unemployed children in the family or as an independent one.

Most of the elderly people were of the strong opinion that the government must create re-employed opportunities for them for the general welfare of the society.

1. Constitutional Provisions and Privileges to Old Aged People

I. Constitutional Provisions: In the Constitution of India, entry 24 in List 111 of Schedule VII deals with the welfare of Labour, including conditions of work, provident funds, liability for workmen's compensation, invalidity and old age pension and other benefits. Further, Article 41 of Directive Principles of State Policy has particular relevance to old age social security. Item No. 9 of the State List and item 20, 23 and 24 of Concurrent List relates to old age pension, social security and social Insurance.

II. Article 41 of Indian Constitution deals with role of state in providing security to the aged. According to this article, "the state shall, within the, limits of its economic capacity and development, make effective provision for securing the right to work, to education and to public assistance in case of unemployment, OLD AGE, sickness and disablement etc.".

2. Ministry Responsible for Welfare of the Aged

Under the Ministry of Social Justice and Empowerment, special care has been taken for the welfare of the older people as under:-

a. National Policy on Older Persons.

b. National Council for older persons. The National Policy has identified a number of areas of intervention such as financial security, health care and nutrition, shelter, protection of life and property and general welfare of the older people in the country. The policy also emphasizes the importance of family in providing non-formal social security to older people.

The National Council has been constituted to operationalise the National Policy to:-

I. Advise the Government on policies and programs for older people,

II. Provide feedback to Government on Policy implementation,

III. Advocate the best interests of older persons,

IV. Provide a nodal agency at the national level for redressing the grievances of older people, and

V. To suggest steps to make old age productive and interesting.

3. Old Age and Income Security

The Ministry also launched a project called "Old Age Social and Income Security" (OASIS) with an objective to evolve and improve a pension system that enables the old people to attain old age security at the price of modest contribution rate through their working career.

4. Privileges and Benefits

a. *Old Age Pension for the General Public: National Old Age Pension Scheme (NOAP):* Under this scheme, central assistance is available on the fulfillment of the following criteria:

   I. The Age of the applicant should be 65 years or more.

   II. The applicant has no regular means of subsistence for his/her own source of income or through financial support from family members or other source.

b. *Annapurna*: Under this scheme, free food grain up to 10 kg per month will be provided to such destitute older persons who are otherwise eligible for old age pension but are not receiving it and whose children are not residing with them.

c. *Income Tax Rebate under section 88B of Finance Act, 1992:* This provision provides rebate of Income Tax to elderly people who has attained the age of 65 years. The tax rebate shall be up to Rs.10,000.

An assesses is entitled to a deduction up to Rs.15,000 if his/her spouse, or dependent parents or any member of the family is an elderly person.

d. *Jeevan Akshay* is a pension plan to provide life long pension and a lump sum death benefit and also a survival benefit at the end of seven years for persons of 50 and above 50 years of age.

e. *Travel Concession*

   I. By Road: 50% discount on fare for travel in big cities like on Delhi Transport Corporation buses and Chandigarh to senior citizens who have attained the age of 65 years.

   II. By train: Indian Railways provide 30% concession in Railway fare for senior citizens.

   III. By Air: 50% discount on adult fare on IA, Sahara, Jet Airways and Domestic flights to senior citizens.

f. Special counters have been earmarked for senior citizens for Railway Ticket Booking, filing Income Tax Returns and paying electricity/ telephone bills, reservation of train, bus seats and, separate OPD in hospitals.

g. *Old Age Homes:* Government has provided Old Age Homes facility also for the elderly persons; There are available free of cost Homes, pay and stay basis old age homes and homes exclusively for women.

Suggestions regarding the state Government's responsibilities towards the welfare of senior citizens.

I. Old age pension must be provided to all the senior citizens above 57 years of age and enhancement of its amount.

II. Supply of necessary commodities at subsidized rates; concession in taxi/bus fare etc.

III. Free medical facilities within and outside the state.

IV. Benefit of centrally sponsored schemes to all the senior citizens.

V. Recognition of elderly persons by inviting them to participate in public meetings and at times honoring them with citation and gifts.

VI. To provide financial assistance for self-entrepreneurship or re-employment.

VII. To set up counseling/training centers for self-help.

VIII. Create awareness among them about the various welfare schemes and its timely implementation.

IX. To set up senior citizen forums as the state, district and village level financed by State Government.

X. To conduct surveys related to socio-economic and health conditions of the older people particularly in remote rural areas.

Elderly people are a reservoir of experience, let us give them love, respect and attention.

You held ours hands when we learn to walk: Now. As you enter the autumn of your life. Society is prepared to hold your hands

REFERENCES

1. *Senior Citizens Guide,* Help Age India, C-14, Qutab Institutional Area, New Delhi.

2. *Help Age India - Research and Development Journal.*

3. *Help Age India - Annual Reports & News.*

4. League, Jacques: Demographic Aspects of the Aging Process - Past and Future Trends, *Synthesis of National Monographic on Population Aging,* India.

5. Ara, Shabeen, *Old Age, Among Slum Dwellers,* South Asia Publishers, 1994, New Delhi.

6. *National Policy on Older Persons, 1999.*

3

AGEING IN NAGALAND: A SOCIOLOGICAL STUDY

—*Visielie*

It is natural that all that are born should grow, and become old and so will human beings. Ageing is a natural and universal phenomenon. It has been defined in various ways by different scholars and measured in many ways according to the academic background of the scholars who have studied them. The concept of the old age is not the same throughout the world. Some have regarded ageing as a period of physiological deterioration, others regard it as the advancement of years and still, others have emphasized that ageing involves a restriction on cultural roles. A chronological definition is often useless, because people who at 65 or 70 years are more vibrant and "youthful" than many people in their thirties or forties. Other definitions of "old" are equally inadequate for specific individuals.

Ageing of an individual is conceived as a perpetual process associated with passage of time. It is unequivocally universal, inevitable and irreversible process of all organisms. In primitive and simple society, a person is considered as old when he attains certain years or age, gets grey hair, wrinkles on the skin, loss of the teeth, eyesight, physical and memory power and has grand-children and so on. In traditional society, transfers of roles and statuses from old to young are clearly marked. The process of changes in roles and responsibilities go on like a cycle in society.

The term gerontology - the scientific study of ageing-has been derived from Greek words '*Geronto*' or '*Geron*' meaning 'old man' and 'logy' meaning 'science'. The science of gerontology is concerned with situations and changes, inherent in increment of time, with particular reference to stages. It is also concerned with changes that occur between the attainment of maturity and death of individual. It is related to the problems of the aged male and female in social group. "*Geriatrics*" is also a combination of the two Greek words namely '*Geron*' meaning 'old man' and '*Latrikos*' meaning 'medical treatment'. This term was coined by an American Physician Ignaz Naschev. It deals with that area of medical practice which is concerned with the psychological and morbidity problems of the aged. According to Ramasubrahmanyam *geriatrics* is a branch of medical science which has to do with age and its diseases (Sahu, 1998: 1).

Social gerontology seeks to discover the role of environment, culture and social change as determinants of ageing and of the behaviour and position of old people as groups and in the aggregate; and their impact on social values and institutions and on economic, political, and social organization, structure and function.

The problem of ageing is, therefore, one that well merits study, both from the point of the individual and from that of the nation. Continued participation of older people in work force and withdrawal from it has become a major interest of social gerontologists. Social gerontologists have been interested in persistence of earlier roles and role changes, activities and life styles in retirement, and in the conceptualization and meaning of leisure to older people.

Dimension of Ageing

Ageing has three inter-related but different connotations namely biological, psychological and socio-cultural. Biological aspect of ageing refers to the identification of multiple biological processes that limits the span of species and individuals or to find out why species and individual members of species have determinates span of life: "Psychological ageing, on the other hand includes the study of psychological capacities, perception, learning, problem solving, feelings, emotions, social behaviour and other related characteristics as they emerge and change consequent upon old age". Social age refers to the social habits and roles of the individual relative to his group or society. Throughout the entire life, human beings live in a social environment. Every society has its own yardstick of comprehending the concept of ageing and age statuses. The age-related roles, privileges and expectations are to a large extent determined by the socio-cultural norms of the society. When a person attains old age, apart from the biological and psychological phenomena, his social role, value orientation, modes of behaviour and expectation undergo rapid changes. These changing social characteristics are not uniform and universal. The social parameters of recognizing a person as an aged vary across cultures, countries, societies and groups.

In any changing society ageing becomes more problematic because it becomes very difficult for the aged to depart from the traditional values and norms and adapt to modern values and norms. In this condition their attitudes toward new functions of society in terms of acceptance or rejection of the new values and norms reflect their reactions to the situation in which they are placed and become relevant to their adjustment. Social gerontology relates to the problems of the aged men and women in a social group. It is a noted fact that becoming old invites various kinds of problems, but attaining 'old-hood' is valuable from the cultural point of view.

Old age is characterized by economic insecurity, ill-health, loneliness, resistance to change and failing physical and mental power. When the aged lose their spouse, friend, job, income or health that cannot be replaced. It brings in them intolerance, rigidity of attitudes, selfishness and suspiciousness. This shift in their psychological make-up makes their living and adjustment in a society more problematic.

Since time immemorial, the Angami Nagas lived in a world of their own. They had their own social structure, culture and socio-economic and political organisation. But the tranquility was disturbed with the advent of the outsider i.e. the British. No doubt, this transition has also broughtforth so many positive changes. However, while accepting new way of life; the Angami Nagas have left behind their traditional way of life, considering it as inferior and outdated. The socio-cultural changes brought about by conversions to Christianity, growth of modern education, new occupations and inculcation of western values, occupational mobility, changing family structure and negative attitudes of the younger generation towards the aged are the main contributing factors to the emerging problem of the old age in the Angami Naga community.

The paper attempts to study a comparative study of the socio-cultural and economic dimensions of the aged, roles and responsibilities accorded to and undertaken by the aged people in the social life of the Angami Naga, changes in the traditional statuses, rights and duties of the aged people as a result of conversion, education, migration, and occupational mobility.

The field site of this study is Kohima town (the capital of Nagaland). Kohima town has been chosen to know whether migration, urbanization and the growth of modern education and occupations have led to the deterioration of the traditional life style of the Angami Nagas. The sources of data include both primary and secondary. The primary sources include personal interviews and observation. The secondary sources are the published works, local newspapers, reports and documents. The stratified random sampling technique was used for selecting the men and women respondents of age 60-year and above. The sample size was of 100 respondents (50 men and 50 women) from ten colonies of the Angami Nagas.

Finding of the Study

There is no complete agreement for the exact age, which can be regarded as cut-off point for determining the aged. Ageing is a natural and universal phenomenon. The sociological aspect of individual ageing is concerned with changes in the circumstances or situations of the individual as a member of the family, community and society. The changes and events associated with include age- grading and social attitudes and behaviour of society toward the ageing individual, completion of parental roles, reduced income, restricted activity and mobility, loss of spouse and associates, large increments of free time and relative absence of clearly defined social expectations.

The major findings covering the socio-economic life are: household composition, living arrangement, migration, age-sex composition and marital status, educational attainment and economic life. The role of the aged in family, religion and medical aspect drawn from the Angami aged in Kohima town the capital of Nagaland and are presented in this presentation.

Household Composition

Eighty-two (82%) of the respondents are living with more than 5 members in a household. In the study 71 (38 males and 33 females) of the aged are married. The study reveals that more men than women. Gender disparity in marital status among elderly is found all over India (Bhaswar, 2001).

This study covers 100 elders who are divided into five age groups 60 years and above. Table 1 shows that the number of married men and women is 71 (38 males and 33 females). The age group of 61-65 has the highest number with 30 married couples (17 males and 13 females). Furthermore, 8 widowers and 14 widows are found in the age group of 61-65 and 76-80 respectively. Three respondents are unmarried of which two are bachelors and one is a spinster, in the age group of 61-65 and in the age group of 66-70.

In the present study the numbers of married males (38) out-number the number of married females (33). Predominance of widows over widowers (8 widowers and 14 widows) is found and the most obvious factor is greater longevity of the women than men. In addition, women tend to marry men older than themselves, and sometimes the age gap in marriage is as 8-10 years, which compounds the likelihood of women outliving their spouses. Further, there is a wider social acceptance of remarriage among widowers than among widows.

In the present study the author came across six types of living arrangements. They are:

(1) Living alone 4% (2 males and 2 females).

(2) Living with spouse 5% (3 males and 2 females).

(3) Living with spouse and unmarried children 37% (20 males and 17 females).

Table 1: Age-Sex Composition and Marital Status

Age Group	Unmarried		Married		Widowers/ Widows		Divorcee		Separated		Total
	Male	Female	Male	Female	Male	Female	Male	Female	Male	Female	
61-65	1	1	17	13	3	4		1			40
66-70	1		6	11	2	3			1		24
71-75			7	6		2					15
76-80			5	3	2	2		1			13
80 and above			3		1	3			1		8
Total	2	1	38	33	8	14		2	2		100

(4) Living with married sons 47% (24 males and 23 females)

(5) Living with married daughters 4% (1 male and 3 females).

(6) Living with grandsons/grand-daughters 3% (3 females).

Educational Attainment

In the traditional Angami society, in every sphere of social activity, there exists a strong sense of competition, be it in the paddy fields, in the jhums, in the feast of merit or in war. Competitions between individuals, groups, clans and villages engage the Angami Naga society. Today the level of competition is high in the field of education between individuals, groups, different clans and different villages.

Table 2: Educational Levels of the Respondents' Parents

Education Level	Respondents' Father	Respondents' Mother	Total (%)
Illiterate	42	46	88
Primary Level	8	4	12
Total	50	50	100

The literacy rate of the respondents' parents shows that out of 8 respondents' father and 4 respondents' mother, 12 (12%) are literate with the primary level of education. Of the 42 respondents' fathers and 46 respondents' mothers, 88 (88%) of the aged parents are illiterate (Table 2).

On the educational level of the respondents Table 3 shows that 36% (15 males and 21 females) are illiterate; one just literate female respondent was also found in the study. Sixty-three per cent (35 males and 28 females) receives formal education. On the whole, it shows that 64% of the Angami aged is literate and 36% (15 males and 21 females) are illiterates.

Table 3: Educational Levels of the Respondents (%)

Educational Level	Male	Female	Total
Illiterate	15	21	36
Literate with no Formal Education		1	1
Primary	10	9	19
Secondary	12	11	23
Pre-University	7	5	12
Graduation	4	3	7
Technical Education			
Diploma in Civil Engineering	1		1
MBBS	1		1
Total	50	50	100

From the comparison of the two tables above, it shows that respondents' parents literacy rate is 12% and the respondents' literacy rate is 64%. This proved that there is an improvement of 52% literacy rate in the field of education within a single generation between respondents' parents and the respondents.

Today, modern education is one of the most important factors that have contributed a tremendous change in the social life of an Angami Naga. It is a contributory factor for moving up the social ladder and recognition of a person's social status.

Migration

According to the *Oxford Dictionary of Sociology,* "Migration involves the permanent movement of individuals or groups across symbolic or political boundaries into new residential areas and communities". With respect to International Migration, the recommendation of the United Nations states removal for one year or more as "Permanent" and thus as migration, while a stay for a shorter period is classified as a "visit" (*International Encyclopedia of the Social Sciences*, Vol 9 & 10: 286).

Majority of the respondents are migrants who have moved to Kohima four to five decades ago. Kohima is the only town in Nagaland inhabited by Angamis, with administrative offices, commercial centers, educational institutions and other employment opportunities. *The International Encyclopedia of the Social Sciences* (Vol. 9 & 10), defines "A person who moves from one home to another in the same neighborhood, and therefore retains the same social framework is not deemed a migrant". However, for the Angamis, to move from 'one home' is moving from 'one village' and to 'same neighborhood' is moving to 'Kohima town'. In Kohima town, majority of the respondents are the 'migrants' from the neighboring villages located at a distance of 10-50 kilometres. It is also interesting that few respondents who are settled in Kohima town are practicing cultivation in their native villages. They leave for their fields around 7:30-8 a.m. and return to Kohima in the evening around 4-5 p.m. No respondent is a native of Kohima town. They maintain regular contacts with their native place. In this way, they maintain strong psycho-physical health even in old age.

Place of Origin

It is significant to know that all the respondents in Kohima Town are rural dwellers who had migrated from nearby/neighboring villages under Angami villages of Kohima District of an Angami inhabited areas. Since time immemorial each Naga tribe concentrated and inhabited one particular area as a dominant tribe, and their identification was based on their village.

The Angamis are divided into four regions which are based on geographical location of its tribe as Northern Angami where Kohima, the capital of Nagaland falls under its jurisdiction, Southern Angami, Western Angami, Chakhro Angami which is presently under Dimapur District. The Angamis are the dominant group of Kohima district till the bifurcation of Dimapur district from Kohima on 28 April 1998. In the study, out of 49 males and 48 females, all have migrated from rural areas to Kohima Town. There were only 3 respondents with migration from urban urban areas. The reason for urban-urban migration is due to transfer of posting.

Soodan (1975) in his work 'Social and Economic Status of the Aged in Lucknow City' reveals that only 18.46% of the aged were drawn from rural areas while 81.54% of the aged live in urban areas. Of the 100% aged in Lucknow city, 39.34 % were born in the city, while 60% had migrated to City from outside. In contrast to the status of the aged in Lucknow, the present study reveals that 100% of the Angami aged were born in the rural areas and migrated to Kohima Town only after the World War II (1945). Though the British shifted their headquarters to Kohima in the year 1878, there was no migrant to Kohima from neighbouring villages. It was only after the Second World War that Angamis from the four regions migrated to Kohima for commercial, educational and employment purposes. In the study none was born and brought up in Kohima Town. This supports the above fact that all the aged are rural migrants and 'Local Movers'. All the respondents are migrants within a district of four regions of an Angami inhabited areas of Northern Angami, Southern Angami, Western Angami and Chakhro Angami regions. In the study 11% were found to have migrated 4-5 decades ago. Nineteen migrated 3-4 decades ago. Forty-one (41%) migrated three decades back and 28 migrated less than 20 years ago.

Five factors of purpose of migration were found in the study the data shows that 8% (5 males and 3 females) have migrated for educational purpose. Forty-nine (49%) (31 males and 18 females) migrated for employment, which is the largest pull-factor for migration in the study. Fifteen (15%) (1 males and 14 females) have migrated on marriage, 24% (9 males and 15 females) have migrated to join family members. Four (4%) (4 males) migrated due to change of residence and all these respondents belong to the native of Kohima village (Table 4).

Table 4: Purpose of Migration

Sl.No.	Purpose	Male	Female	Total
1	Education	5	3	8
2	Employment	31	18	49
3	Marriage	1	14	15
4	To Joint Family Members	9	15	24
5	Others	4		4
	Total	50	50	100

Majority of the respondents' own properties like land, forest, house, paddy field, cattle etc. in their native place. Thirteen (13%) owned no land in their native place. Forty-four (44%) of the respondents are getting some sources of income from property in their native place. The major sources are by selling forest products like bamboos, firewood, timber, paddy and terrace cultivation, and farm products like fruits and green vegetable. Fifty-nine (59%) is not getting any Income from their property, of this 46% properties are operated by their family members and relatives without any tax and 13% own no property.

Frequency of Visits to Native Places

Of the 100 respondents, 85 (85%) pay regular visits to their native place once or twice in a year. Out of these 85, 36% is for visiting relatives, 6% to supervise agriculture, 13 to participate in church activities and only 25% to participate in the village council meeting. In the analysis of this 25 (25%) most of these are retired Government servants, businessmen, social workers and educated persons who held position and status in the society. Five visit their native place without any specific purpose. Sixteen never visited their native place for the last several years, as they are too old to travel for long distance.

The data show that 84% are frequently in contact with their native place and 16% never visit at all. Of this 84%, 23% visit weekly, 28% visit once or twice a month, 33% visits once or twice in a year.

Economic Life

The Angami Nagas in the past were more or less self-sufficient. Villages had their own cultivable land sufficient to support their own population, livestock for meat and a wide range of forest areas around the villages for getting building materials, firewood, etc. The forest also served as hunting grounds for hunting wild animals and for food gathering. In other words, the villagers were economically self-sufficient to meet their simple living.

Sources of Income

The respondents have seven sources of income; they are salary, rent from property, interest on savings, profit from business, government pension, old age pension and others. The study reveals that 38 (38%) are retired Govt. employees. 23 (23%) are getting income from property. Eleven (11%) are engaged in business. Four (4%) have income from their earnings of which two are employed in church services and the other two are in private sector. Nine (9%) are getting Old Age Pension, as their only source. Seven (7%) have no source of their own.

Table 5: Sources of Monthly Income

Sl.No.	Sources	Male	Female	Numbers
1	Salary	3	1	4
2	Rent from Property	12	11	23
3	Interests on Savings	2	3	5
4	Profit from Business	3	9	11
5	Govt. Pension	24	14	38
6	Old Age Pension	4	5	9
7	Others	2	5	7
	Total	50	50	100

Acharya and Das (1989) in their study of aged Chasa Kandhas of Phulbani district in Orissa reveal that only 52% of the aged are earners whereas the rest (48%) do not have any source of income. The aged who earns depend upon property, wages, and begging as a major source. In the present study of the Angami aged in Kohima town, 93% of the aged are getting income from some sources as against 52% of the aged of Chasa Kandhas tribes. Income sources from wages and begging is not prevalent among the Angami aged in Kohima town, but it was found among the Chasa Kandhas tribe. The parameter of income alone cannot determine the status of a person in an Angami society. Because since time immemorial prestige has given to land, paddy, forest, cattle, etc.

Table 6: Earners and Non-Earners

Status of the Respondents	Male	Female	Total
Chief Bread Earners	34	19	53
Part-time Earners	14	26	40
Non-Earners	2	5	7
Total	50	50	100

In the study of 100 elders, 53 (34 males and 19 females) (53%) are the chief bread earners in the family (Table 6). Forty (14 males and 26 females) (40%) are part-time earners. Seven (2 males and 5 females) (7%) do not have any sources of income and are wholly dependent on their children and grandchildren for their survival.

From the above data, three inferences can be drawn. Firstly, exercise of authority by the aged is governed largely by their economic status. The higher the earning status, the higher is the exercise of authority, the lower the earning status, lower is the exercise of authority. Secondly, the majority of the aged who exercise high and medium authority in the family are chief bread earners. Thirdly, in the case of aged exercising low authority or no authority at all, the majority are part-time earners followed by non-earners.

Therefore, one can assume that the loss of economic status results in a reduced status in relation to their children to some extent, but it does not result in loss of authority for a majority of the aged. In community affairs middle aged people play a dominant role and older people are relegated into the background. The forces of urbanization, industrialization and education etc. have made the status of the aged problematic in comparison to traditional societies. Therefore, an attempt has been made in the present study to examine the status, prestige, authority, power and security.

Occupation

There has been occupational mobility between respondents' parents, respondents' occupation and the respondents' children occupation. This is because the table shows that only 6% of the respondents' parents were employed whereas 67% of the respondents are employed against this 92% of the respondents' children are employed. Ninety-four (94%) of the respondents' parents were depending on agriculture as their main occupation while 33 (33%) of the respondents are depending on agricultural occupation, whereas only 8% of the respondents' children are practicing agriculture as their main occupation. This clearly shows that as a result of conversion, migration, modern education and urbanization there has been a drastic change in the occupations of the respondents and their parents.

The respondents have served in all the four classes. Under class I category, eight (8%) (5 males and 3 females) have served as sub-divisional officer (SDO), under secretary, director, and superintendent. In class II, 4 (4%) (2 males and 2 females) have served as officers like assistant engineer, assistant superintendent, laboratory assistant, and steno. In class-III category, 16 (16%) (11 males and 5 females) have worked as lower divisional assistant (LDA), upper divisional assistant (UDA), inspector, clerk, and constable. Under class IV, 10 (10%) (6 males and 4 females) have worked as peon, driver, sweeper, and chowkidar.

In the traditional Angami society where people depended on agriculture for their livelihood, the aged were actively engaged in the social, economic, political, and the religious activities. And there was no retirement for the aged because status and prestige were accorded to them on the basis of age, wisdom and experience in the society. In the present society, as a result of modern education, migration, and occupational mobility there are far more employment opportunities, where status and prestige are associated with their educational level and income. So, from the analysis of the study it can be concluded that disengagement theory is the result of migration, conversion, education and urbanization.

Financial Assistance from Children

Although property and personal savings are important sources of income, assistance from children constitutes another important source of income for the Angami aged. Twenty-nine (29%) are getting financial assistance from their children regularly. Nineteen (19%) are getting assistance occasionally, and 31 (31%) get on specific occasions such as Father's Day, Mother's Day, Christmas and other important occasions. Twenty (20%) are not getting any assistance. Data show that 10 respondents (10%) are getting Rs.100-500 every month from their children, four (4%) get between Rs.501-1000, six (6%) get between Rs.1001-1500, and two (2%) get between Rs.1501-2000; and only 4(4%) get 2000 and above.

There are two schemes of Old Age Pension. They are: (1) National Old Age Pension for 65-plus age group and (2) State Old Age Pension for 70-plus age group where prescribed conditions of eligibility relating to age apply. In the study it was found that only 28 respondents are getting old age pension (Table 7).

Table 7: Beneficiaries of Old Age Pension in Nagaland and the Study Area (Kohima Town)

Old Age Beneficiaries	Nagaland		Kohima Town		Study Area	
	No. of 60+	Benefi-ciaries	No. of 60+	Benefi-ciaries	No. of Aged 60+	Benef-iciaries
State Old Age Pension (70+)	8882		1952		13	
National Old Age Pension (65+)	27,408		3346		15	
Total						

Source: Office of the Director of Social Welfare, Nagaland, Kohima, 2001.

The Role of the Aged in the Family

Family occupies a unique position in the human society. As a social institution, family fulfils the need and interests of the large number of individuals as compared to any other social institution. In general, an individual is born in the family, brought up in the family, grows old in the family, and in normal course dies in the family.

The joint family system cannot operate among the Nagas as they are very much independent minded people, and detest depending on others for their livelihood (Horam, 1998). This is amply proved by the fact that in the traditional Naga society - still found in most Naga villages and also practised by the Angami Nagas - as soon as the sons are married, they move out from their parents' house. Another house is built for the parents among the Sema and the Thangkhul Nagas. Nagas never had the joint family system. Familism is deeply rooted and this bond is very strong. The sons and relatives look after the old parents and invalids. If, for instance, a member of the family has fallen sick or facing an adversity, the members come forward and help him out of his plight.

In the study area many of the Angami aged are living in nuclear families with their unmarried sons and daughters eventhough their married sons have left their families. The position of the aged in the family is not much affected by the departure of married sons leaving behind unmarried brothers and sisters, for the parents continue to manage the family affairs and shoulder the responsibility as before. Education of children, occupational mobility and migration have brought changes in the family system and consequently challenged the authority of the aged people. They feel hurt when their children refer to them as old fashioned and outdated. As a result of modem education and economic independence, children have become more vocal in the sustenance of the family.

Majority of the respondents in the study area are early risers and they spend time in a variety of ways.

91 respondents (91%) take part into different activities daily. Nine (9%) are not able to move outside the house. Nearly 50 respondents (48%) of the respondents are assisting by their children in the household activities such as cleaning house, cooking, washing clothes, purchased of household provisions and entertaining guest. Almost 22 (22%) are found working together with their children. Sixteen (16%) serve by the respondents themselves. Fourteen (14%) assisting by their servants.

An attempt to find out the pattern of utilization of free time by the respondents has revealed the respondents spend their leisure time in various ways such as gossip and discussions (9%), going for a stroll (9%), watching television (14%), visiting friends (16%), visiting Church (15%), reading books (8%) and by playing with their grand-children (18%) and 7% spend their leisure time by watching people on the street. Thus, majority of the respondents are spending their free time in gossiping and discussion, and there are no places such as '*Thehuba*' or youth dormitories in Kohima Town where the aged can tell the folktales and stories for healthy and satisfactory use of free time as in the traditional Angami society. This opportunity is missing today.

Forty-nine of the respondents (49%) have participated in decisions making at the household level like 'searching girls for boys/boys for girls.' The respondents have also taken decision pertaining to children's education and occupation. Twenty-one respondents (21%) have participated in decisions making at the neighborhood or colony levels. Nineteen respondents (19%) participate in decision-making at the 'Clans' and 'Village' levels and 11 respondents never participated in any kind of decisions related to family, farm or at the village levels.

Participation in Religious Activities

In the study, 44 respondents (44%) spend 3-6 hours per week for church activities. Eighteen (18%) spend

10-15 hours a week all are females and they have weekly separate service for women. Nine (9%) serves as the church workers and spend their time depending upon the church activities. Twenty nine (29%) could not give their comments.

Sixty-eight (68%) attend Sunday worship service regularly. Thirteen (13%) attend Sunday worship service once or twice every month. Eleven (11 %) attend Church once or twice in a year. From the above we can draw that 71 (30 males and 41 females) (71%) attend Church regularly on every Sunday. This shows that women are more religious than men. Five (5%) never attend Sunday services at all, two are still following non-Christian religion and three respondents are difficult to attend church activities on health ground.

Table 8: Assistance from the Church

Age Groups	Regularly/ Monthly	Occasion-ally	On Specific Occasions	Not Getting Assistance	Total
61-65	2	14	11	13	40
66-70	1	10	9	4	24
71-75		6	8	1	15
76-80	2	3	7	1	13
80 and above	1	2	5		8
Total	6	35	40	19	100

The frequencies of getting assistance from the Church are divided into four categories (Table):

1. On regular/monthly basis,
2. Occasionally,
3. Specific occasions and
4. Not getting assistance.

The types of assistance are found in form of concerns, prayer support, monetary, clothings, firewood, vegetables, etc. received from the Church.

In the modern Angami Naga society, with the majority of the population being Christians, today many of the festivals are celebrated without rituals. As Christianity is not biased towards any individual or a particular sex, both men and women freely participate in all religious ceremonies.

Angami Women

In the traditional society, 'women', whether as wife, daughter, sister or mother were made to feel inferior to men. As a wife/mother, she was in charge of the household chores but in other matters she was subjected to consult her husband. Both male and female worked together, ate together and sought suggestions from each other in the functioning of the family. But in matters of decision making it was male who always give the final word, 'yes' or 'no' or either to 'agree' or to 'disagree'.

This scenario has taken a U-turn in the modem society. With the growth of literacy rate, the social attitude towards women has broadened a great deal. The Western norm of equality has made a fissure in the tight compartments of male and female differences in our society. Education has made many a mother and wife earners, which has raised the women's moral and social standing. The wife or mother need not necessarily confine herself to the household drudgery, but is free to engage her in other social and economic matters as her competency and abilities render her fit. Today, education is encouraged for both sexes, which has helped in raising the status of women in general.

Health and Medical Care

In the study of 100 elders 95 respondents (95%) are having health problem and only 5 (5%) are free from ailments. Blood Pressure, arthritis, diabetes, liverish, backache, giddiness, constipation, asthma, indigestion, toothache, gastrointestinal and others, with varying degree of affliction are some of the physical disorders from which the respondents are suffering which are observed among the aged.

Systems of Medical Treatment

Table 9 shows the systems of medical treatment accessible by the aged.

Table 9: Systems of Medical Treatment

Sl.No.	Types of Medical treatment	Males	Females	Total
1	Private allopathic doctor	7	5	12
2	Govt. Clinic/Hospitals	14	19	33
3	Indigenous Practice	13	14	27
	Any Other	16	12	28
	Total			100

Thirty-three go to Government Clinics/Hospitals. Twenty-seven use indigenous medicines and 28 have never visited the health centers or private practitioners for treatment. Forty-five (45%) respondents have access to medical treatment. These respondents are economically sound and are getting financial assistance from their children. Twenty-seven (27%) uses indigenous medicine because they cannot afford expensive medication. Another reason is the belief among the aged that such complaints are common phenomenon among the aged. Out of twenty eight (28%) respondents who have never used any kind of treatment, 17 (17%) say that it is a common experience that out-patients department in every hospital or dispensary are much over crowded and aged persons have to wait for long hours to get their turn to be attended by the doctor. Thus, majority of the aged refrain from visiting them unless it becomes unavoidable and others say that they feel disgusted and frustrated and lose interest in taking care of their life.

Fifty-six respondents (56%) stay at home during illness. Twenty-four (24%) stay at hospitals. Seventeen (17%) stay at their children places, and 3 females' (3%) stays at their grandchildren's place. At the time of illness, 78 respondents (78%) are taken care by their children and family members, 13 (13%) by their grandchildren and 11 (11%) by their relatives. All those who take care by their relatives are widows and widowers living alone and an unmarried bachelor.

Changing Status of the Aged

The basic changes in the family system of modem society have taken place as a result of the shift from rural/agricultural setting to an urban/industrial setting. In the traditional or agricultural society, experience is most important for functioning of the society. Since experience accumulates with increasing age, old persons are accorded position of high prestige and respect. In contrast, modern industrial society is characterized by rapid technological progress and new experiences while the past experiences of the aged have lost much of their value. As a consequence, the decreasing importance of experience is reflected in the loss of status and respect for the aged. Moreover, there is also a shift from an authoritarian-patriarchal type of family to an equalitarian partnership system, reflected in the fact that the child of today has become more independent. The relationship between the child and the parents is now more informal and children carry more weight in decision making within the family.

In this study, an attempt was also made to know that either woman should involve in all decision pertaining to family matters. Thirty-three respondents (33%) agree that women should be involved in decision making pertaining to all family matters. Fifty-three (53%) are disagreeing to it, while 14 (14%) say it can be considered an exceptional case. From the analysis it is found that females have more patriotic feeling of traditional customs of the Angami Nagas than to males, because majority of the females agree with endocentric or male control.

The Angami Nagas are passing through a transitional phase, they are adapting to new ways of life, disregarding their age-old ways. Along with the human race, today Angami Naga is also caught up in a world of revolution, which is so dynamic and powerful that it has become almost out of human control. There is no aspect of the Angami Naga life, which has not been touch by change. Whether we look at the economically, politically, socially or in the religious field, many changes have taken place.

Traditionally, aged were the responsibility of the family and society in the Angami Naga society. However, gradual breaking down of this system over the last few years has left the aged unprotected. It is evident that modern living conditions, the attitudes of the young towards the old have undergone a significant change due to higher education, economic mobility, and urban areas. The demographic changes in family structure due to urbanization and industrialization have resulted in changes in other aspects of family like sentiments, behavioral patterns and attitude.

Though most of the children are living away from their aged parents, the existence of mutual help in several ways is still observed between generations. This exchange involves the services such as household maintenance, financial assistance and help in kind like clothes, food materials and so on. It is found that the exchange is more or less a reciprocal gesture. Though most of the aged expressed that they prefer 'giving' to 'taking' and that they are reluctant to accept assistant from their children, primarily material help, for fear of jeopardizing their mutual relations. But many circumstances force them to compromise to this stand.

It is not easy for old people who cannot climb steps, walk long distances, and travel in overcrowded buses to reach most of the hospitals in rural and urban care centers. It is high time that health care for the elderly is arranged periodically in their home.

From the above analysis the following suggestions are given for the care of the aged:

(1) The status, role and privileges of the aged are looked down in the present Angami Naga society; that there is a need for setting up Old Age Home to meet the basic needs of the aged.

(2) Policy for the care of the elderly in their respective homes should be introduced. (3) Since social status of the aged mostly depend on their economic status, increasing Old Age Pension schemes by the state government may help them in improving their socio-economic status.

(4) Lastly, setting up of subsidized health care for the aged with separate geriatric units in every hospitals with free or highly subsidized medicine.

Elderly Persons are the best Advisors and Consultants in Society

REFERENCES

1. Acharya and P.K. Das (1989), Socio-Economic Status and Health condition of the Aged Tribals of Phulbani, Orissa'. In: R.N. Pati and B. Jena (eds.), *Aged in India*. New Delhi: Ashish Publishing House.

2. Bhawsar, Rahul, Dev (2000), 'Population Ageing in India: Demographic and Health Dimensions'. In: Modi, Ishwar (ed.), *Ageing and Development*. Jaipur: Rawat Publications.

3. Bhatia, H.S. (1983), *Aging and Society*, Udaipur: Aryas Book Centre.

4. Crandal, R.C. (1980), *Gerontology: A Behavioural Science Approach*, U.S.A.: Adison-Wesley Publishing Co.

5. Dandekar, K. (1996), *The Elderly in India*, New Delhi: Sage Publications.

6. Horam, M. (1998), *Nagas Old Ways New Trends*, New Delhi: Cosmo Publications.

7. Hutton, J.H. (1968), *The Angami Nagas*, Bombay: Oxford University Press.

8. Sahu, C. (1998), *Problems of Ageing among the Indian Tribes*, New Delhi: Sarup and Sons.

9. Soodan, Kirpal Singh. (1975), *Aging in India*, Calcutta: Minerva Associate Publications.

10. Srivastava (1994), *The Problem of the Old Age*, New Delhi: Classical Publishing Co.

11. *International Encyclopaedia of Social Sciences*, Vol. 9 & 10.

4

PROBLEMS OF OLD AGED AND THE NEED FOR CARE: A CASE STUDY OF MOKOKCHUNG TOWN

—A. Lanunungsang

Introduction

Aged persons are special who need special attention and care. Their silent language and cry should not be left unheard. This is a piece of work undertaken in Mokokchung town taking 106 samples as a case study to project the problems of aged people and the need for care.

Mokokchung town is a beautiful hill station, the second largest hill town in the state after Kohima, the state capital. This town is the district administrative headquarters founded by the British administrators during 19th century in the process of annexation of Naga territory in the region.

Accordingly, in the year 1888, the Ao country was annexed by the British occupational force and beginning from that year, Mokokchung became their administrative headquarters for various reasons such as centrality of the Eastern Region, easy accessibility from Assam and gateway to Eastern Border reaching Burma. It was created as a sub-division in 1957 and upgraded to a district status having three satellite stations namely Mokokchung, Wokha and Zunheboto. In the year 1973, Wokha and Zunheboto were made separate districts. Being strategically situated, Mokokchung is the gateway to Tuensang and Zunheboto districts and also to Eastern corridor via Tuensang district reaching Myanmar. Situated at a height of 1,325 metres above the mean sea level, the climate is extremely pleasant throughout the year.

Mokokchung town is the cultural headquarters of the Ao community. The birth of modern education and religion turned this town as a centre of new civilization in the state. The town is surrounded by many historical villages with beautiful tourist spots and other rural institutions. The most prominent villages that are located near this town are Ungma, Khensa, Chuchuy-imbang, Chungtia, Aliba, Changki, Mopungchuket, Sangratsu etc. including the Ao Baptist Church head-quarters at Impur nearby Mokokchung town. This town is populated by many elderly people mostly from those surrounding villages. Apart from the Aos, people of different communities have migrated tc this town for various purposes such as education, business, health care, economic and domestic interests. Thus, this town is the home of elderly people though many of the educated and affluent elderly Ao people have migrated to Dimapur and Kohima towns since eighties and nineties of the last century.

The whole district is divided into 8 administrative units headed by Additional Deputy Commissioner/Extra Assistant Commissioner respectively. The district is divided into 6 distinct ranges which are lying parallel to each other. There are about 100 government recognized villages, 6 developmental blocks, 3 sub-divisions and 9 administrative circles. The total population of the town is about 35-40 thousand.

The town administration is divided into 16 wards. There is a strong administrative networking system of the town headed by Ward Chairman who is assisted by a number of nominated elderly people representing different original villages and ranges. The election to the Town Municipal Board in all the major towns in the state have already been conducted but the residents of Mokokchung town are still hesitating to elect the members of the Town Municipal Board mainly due to objection raised by the landowners of the surrounding villages. However, in the line of other towns administration in the state, Mokokchung town Municipal Board is also coming up gradually. This town represents the character of urban society in Nagaland.

Method

For the purpose of this study, we have randomly identified 106 aged people ranging from 62 years and above from different wards. The required information has been collected through a questionnaire schedule prepared as tool for data collection. One field investigator was engaged for one week for collection of the data contained in this paper. First of all, the data were transferred from questionnaire schedule to the master tabulation sheet and entered in the respective tables. The analysis, results and findings are furnished from Table 1.

Table 1: Distribution of Age Structure

Age Range	Male	Female	Total
62-72	36	25	61(64.66%)
72-82	18	14	32(33.92%)
82-92	7	4	11(17.60)
92 & above	2	0	02(2.12%)
Total	63(66.78%)	43(45.58%)	106(100%)

The age structure shown in Table 1 indicates 63 (66.78%) male and 43 (54.58%) female. It covers the age group of 62 to 92 and above of which 93 (98.58%) are below 82 years and hardly 13 (13.78%) constitutes 92 years and above. It shows that elderly persons in Mokokchung town are very few in number.

As stated above, Mokokchung town is a home of elderly people from different communities other than the Aos. In our sample, the age group starts from 62 years and above that ends in 109 years. There were hardly 10 people who have reached 100 years and above. They are mostly from different surrounding villages in the district who came to this town for various reasons and settled down permanently. Out of 106 respondents, 30 people have migrated to this town before the statehood in 1963 and the rest came only after the statehood. In fact, 75 of them have been staying up to 25 years in Mokokchung, 45 of them up to 50 years and 30 persons have completed 50 years and above. Out of 106, 100 are Aos and only 6 respondents belong to other communities other than the Aos.

Table 2: Ward-wise Distribution of the Respondents

S.No.	Name of ward	No. of respondents	%
1.	Alempang	5	4.71
2.	Arkong	11	10.37
3.	Dilong	5	4.71
4.	Kumlong	35	33.00
5.	Marep	5	4.17
6.	Medical	5	4.71
7.	Sangtemla	5	4.71
8.	Surrounding villages	35	33.00
	Total	106	100.00

Out of 16 wards, we have selected only 8 wards. From five wards, we have selected only five respondents each, 11 from Arkong ward and 35 each from Kumlong ward and another 35 from the surrounding villages as indicated in Table 2.

In order to measure their economic problems, their sources of income such as monthly salary, monthly pension, old age pension, house rent including other sources were assessed. In this, 55 of them (51.88%) were never in government service and the rest 51 (48.11%) were found to be retired persons from different categories such as teachers, ex-servicemen, medical professionals and others. They were mostly grade III and IV staff category of the employees. That is why majority of the respondent falls under the income group of Rs. 5,000 per month.

Table 3: Level of Income

Range in Rupees	No. of respondents		Total (%)
	Male	Female	
Below 5000	55	40	95 (89.62)
5,000-10,000	5	4	09 (08.49)
10,000-15,000	1	Nil	01 (00.94)
15,000 above	1	Nil	01 (00.94)
Total	62	44	106

No housing problem is identified among the respondents because most of them are living in their own houses. Since Mokokchung is the cultural headquarters of the Aos, they have their own houses including rented buildings and running shops. Except five respondents, no one of them live in rented house. It shows that there is no housing problem among the elderly people of this town.

Cent per cent of our respondents are married. From the families of 106, begat 560 children and 1301 grandchildren (Table 4). It shows that they are highly productive. The size of the family is recorded to be 5.28 persons per family and most of them can provide living rooms and space to their children and grand children.

Table 4: Marital Status of the Respondents

Married	Un-married	No. of children	No. of grand children	Total
106	Nil	560	1301	1967

Old Age Pension

There are two categories of old age pension viz. State Old Age Pension and National Old Age Pension schemes available in the country. Any person from 70 years and above is entitled to get State Old Age Pension @ Rs. 100 per month, and 65 years and above are entitled to get National Old Age Pension @ Rs. 75 per month. According to latest official record, 1,800 get State Old Age Pension and 3900 people get National Old Age Pension in Mokokchung district. In our sample hardly 17.92% (Table 5) enjoy the facility of old age pension in the district.

Table 5: Status of Old-aged Pension

Availing old age pension or not	Yes	No
Male	08 (7.54%)	50 (47.16%)
Female	11 (10.37)	37 (34.90%)
Total	19 (17.92%)	87 (82.07%)

It is reported that most of the deserving elderly persons are not getting such facility. This may be due to lack of education and un-awareness Many of the most deserving cases are left out especially in rural areas due to lack of information. It is also reported that selection of beneficiary is done on the basis of political party affiliation. Because of such tendency, discrimination continues in every level. The poor and unreached people are neglected.

It was necessary to examine the status of spouses as to whether both of them are still alive or not. Table 6 shows that in the family of 106, 81 (76.41%) both husband and wife are still alive between the age group of 62 years and above. Eighteen (17%) husbands have already expired out of 106 married couples whereas only 7 (06.60%) wife have expired against 18 (76.41%) male members. It indicates that more male members die earlier than their wives in Mokokchung town. And the longevity of both husband and wife is still very strong as indicated in the table below.

Table 6: Status of Husband and Wife who are still Alive or Expired

No. of both husband and wife still alive	No. of wife already expired	No. of husband already expired
81 (76.41%)	07 (06.60%)	18 (17.00%)

Status of Physical Health and Socio-psychological Problem

Table 7 indicates a picture of the status of physical health problems faced by the old aged people in Mokokchung town. Maximum number of respondents (83.96%) suffers from joint pain/ache, followed by cataract problem (39.62%), ulcer/dysentery problem (35.84%), urinary problem (28.30%), asthmatic problem (17.92%), diabetes problem (16.03%) and hearing problem (14.15%). Hardly 3.77% have low blood pressure against 7.54 high blood pressure. Relatively, as compared to their age factor, elderly people of Mokokchung town maintain better health than many other places in other urban areas.

Table 7: Status of Physical Health Problems of Old Aged People in Mokokchung

Nature of problem	Yes			No.		
	Male	Female	Total	Male	Female	Total
Arthritis	Nil	Nil	0	62	44	106
Cataract	28	14	42(39.62)%	35	29	64
Diabetes	13	4	17(16.03)%	13	40	53
Joint pain/ache	50	39	89(83.96)%	12	5	17
Asthmatic	14	5	19(17.92)%	49	38	78
Urinary	25	5	30(28.30)%	37	39	76
Ulcer/dysentery	18	20	38(35.84%)	44	24	68
Piles	4	1	05(4.71%)	58	43	103
Physically handicap	1	2	03(02.83%)	61	42	103
Hearing problem	11	4	15(14.15%)	51	40	91
Low blood pressure	2	2	04(3.77%)	Nil	Nil	0
High blood pressure	6	2	08(7.54%)	Nil	Nil	0
Cardiac	3	Nil	03(02.83%)	Nil	Nil	0

Apart from physical problems, elderly people normally suffer from a number of socio-psychological problems as mentioned in table eight below. All these types of problems have been experienced by elderly people of different societies of the world. They are listed below in Table 8.

Table 8: Status of Socio-psychological Problems

Sl.No.	Types of problem	Yes	No	Total
1.	Loneliness	15	91	106
2.	Depression	8	98	106
3.	Frustration	4	102	106
4.	Aggression	6	100	106
5.	Mental	4	102	106
6.	Dementia	0	106	106
7.	Ill-behaviour	0	106	106
8.	Mis-adjustment	13	93	106
9.	Non-fulfilment	1	105	106
10.	Family disputes	1	105	106
11.	Alcoholism	0	106	106
12.	Divorce	2	104	106

It is good to note that none of the respondents is suffering from dementia, ill-behaviour of the family members and alcoholism. Only one each of the respondent is identified with the problems of non-fulfilment of their requirement and family disputes. Two of the respondents are divorced and four each are found to be suffering from frustration and mental problem. The maximum types of problem are said to be loneliness (14.15%), followed by mis-adjustment (12.26%) and depression 7.54% respectively. The problems of loneliness, mis-adjustment and depression are correlated.

Psychologist opines that cause of depression may be of both biological and psychosocial factors. Various electrochemical conditions of the neural system are known to precipitate depression in some individuals. Among them are, imbalance of chemical substance (neurotransmitters) that carry electrical impulses from one nerve cell to another. When one of these substances known as norepinephrine is subnormally present in an elderly person, that person is likely to be depressed. Many of the elderly people are known to be depressed by the subnormal presence of norepinephrine.

Psychosocial causes are many and varied depending upon the individuals and his environment which includes his past as well the present environment. Poor health (mostly for men), retirement from a cherished vocation, death of the spouse, and financial insecurity (mostly for women) are some of the many psychosocial causes.

Successful Aging

Successful aging depends mostly on the art of living. Living healthy, living happily, living cheerfully, eating and working accurately are some of the indicators of successful aging. Successful aging needs to be taught and learn by every elderly person.

There are three theories of successful living. They are the theory of **own personality**, the theory of **disengagement** and the **theory of activities**. Theory of own personality is sub-divided into a) integrated type who use to reorganize themselves and involve in a wide range of activities. b) Focus theory engages in moderate level of activity being selective in their involvement and c) the successful disengaged theory maintains low activity level and high life satisfaction. The disengagement theory is a gradual withdrawal from active engagement, voluntary retirement from social activities, like compulsory retirement. This theory has been controversial among the gerontologists. Not all the elderly persons are interested in disengagement but definitely there are some who would like to disengage from their occupation.

Activity theory suggests that the aging individuals want to remain productive and active, especially for those persons who were rather active in their middle age, to be disengaged is a great martyrdom and they by all means, want to be of service to the society. They keep busy and engage themselves elsewhere that saves them from boredom.

Outing, home visitation, active participation in religious organizations and socio-cultural spheres are the examples of active theory. If an aged person wants to be happy, he or she must choose the active theory of aged persons. In many other societies especially in urban areas; many elderly persons are mostly confined inside the rooms. As a result, they develop symptoms of artificial neurosis and faster aging.

In Naga society, especially in rural areas, many of the aged persons go to the field every day. They work ceaselessly throughout the day and live a hard life eating hard food that keeps them healthier and stronger. Eating and drinking without daily exercise or doing at least a piece of work regularly makes a person age faster. That is not a successful aging.

Some Suggestions

In a place like Naga society, following suggestions are made for consideration.

1. There is a need to establish **Old Aged Home** in every town in Nagaland creating at least minimum facilities such as free medical check up, counselling, social recreation with spiritual touch;

2. In the villages, the system of **Semtu** or **Salang** in different *khels* should be revived adding modern facilities such as TV, rural telephone

network, play games, traditional crafts making and medical check up from time to time;

3. The churches can play the most vital role meeting the psychosocial and physical needs of the elderly persons. There is a need to create a Special Cell for old aged people in every local church;

4. Old Age Pension should be given to every deserving individual irrespective of political party affiliation, rural and urban dwellers and men and women. For this purpose, awareness education programs may be required and adequate budget should be made available with the concerned state department/authority.

5. Proper arrangement for issue of Old Aged Certificate should be maintained by the competent authority.

6. Since a new department of women has already created by the State Government of Nagaland, this department should provide special facilities to the elderly people of the state.

Let us not forget that the elderly person wants to be listened to the topics of their interest and not ours. Lending a listening ear is highly appreciated by the elderly people. Let us take care of them all.

The Older You Grow Old, Hold on to Your Spouses Tighter.

5

SOCIO-ECONOMIC STATUS OF THE AGED AMONG THE ANGAMI NAGAS

—*Ketshukietuo Dzüvichü*

Notwithstanding the differences in the criteria of defining old age, there has been a great transformation in the structure of society. This paper here makes an attempt to examine the socio-economic problems of the aged among the Angami Nagas. A study of the social status of the aged involves, among others, an analysis of their age and marital status, educational level, living arrangement and occupation. To understand the economic status of the aged their income, source of income, income of the family he lives in, and assets and liabilities are considered. The study reveals that the Angami aged still enjoy higher status in the society. On the economic status, self sufficiency in terms of food availability which is the top priority in an Angami society is prominent but in terms of income, most of them are in the lower income group.

With the progress of life towards the old age, an individual's mental and physical capacity to perform certain roles gradually gets declined, and when he retires from bread-winning stage he has to experience several socio-economic and psychological problems within the family and society. In an industrialised society, according to Rekha Dutt (1986), the knowledge, experience and skills of the older people do no longer relate to the present. The importance of their functional position thus declines, and consequently their authority and much of the respect and prestige they enjoyed earlier gets faded. This change brings frustration and anxieties to older people.

In our traditional social system, old age was generally considered wisdom personified the fruit of a well spent life and often commanded unquestionable power, authority and respect. Looking after the old was taken for granted. The aged could disengage themselves from life and yet retain their position of respect. An attitude of reverence towards the aged was considered a virtue and nothing important could take place in the family without the sanction and blessing of the old.

In modern society, old age is no more what it once used to be but a period entered with reluctance and trepidation and crossed with countless hurdles. A multiplicity of factors contributes to the changing status of the aged in society. In a competitive society where usefulness is measured by economic yardstick, the aged is sometimes considered useless. The rapidity in technological advancement and its accompanying social and cultural change bewilders an aged person's attempts to grapple with it. As a result, old people are today faced with a number of social, economic and psychological problems, which need to be understood in order to devise any comprehensive programme for the welfare of the aged.

Area of Study

The Angami Nagas, one of the major tribes of Nagaland, live in the southern part of Nagaland, i.e., Kohima District. The total area of the district, according to 1991 census, is 4041 square kilometres. The district is bounded by Zunheboto and Phek districts on the east, Assam on the west, Wokha on the north and

Manipur on the south. Their territory is, administratively divided into four regions:

1) Northern Angami,
2) Southern Angami,
3) Western Angami, and
4) Chakhro Angami.

According to the 1991 Census, it has a population of 387,581 persons, and an aged population (60+) of 14,138. The present study is concentrated on four villages, selecting the nearest villages located in all the four directions from the Kohima Town, the State Capital of Nagaland, which are Kohima village, Phesama village, Jotsoma village and Piphema village.

Methodology

The universe of the present study is the aged population (60+) among the Angami Nagas, living in the Kohima District of Nagaland. The data have been collected from four villages in Kohima District. The aged population in this district is found to be 3.6% of the total population. So the total sample size is 380, which is 3.6% of the total population of the four villages. By using the multi-stage sampling design, first the Angami region has been classified (stratified) into four categories (each region forming a stratum). Then the nearest village from Kohima town in each of the four Angami regions in four directions has been selected. As for the aged population they have been stratified into four strata. Literate Male, Illiterate Male, Literate Female and Illiterate Female. Out of the total sample size 280 respondents are from Kohima village, 44 from Phesama village, 42 from Jotsoma Village and 14 from Piphema Village, making use of such device as stratification and sampling with "probability proportionate to size". The sampling units are then further selected by applying systematic sampling, selecting every k[th] aged on the list for each village.

The socio-economic status of the aged is studied on the basis of parameters like rented house or owned, employed or unemployed, education, economically independent or dependent, sources of income, assets and liabilities.

A. Social Status of the Aged

The aged population of the Angami as shown by this study covers a diverse group of people. There are among them those who are just-turned 60 and are still keen on earning a living and supporting themselves and their families. There are single and married people, well-to-do as well as penniless individuals depending upon others for their essential needs. There are people who are healthy and look for relaxation after a long active life and others not so healthy and waiting, as it were, for death to rescue them from the worldly miseries. These characteristics, which have a bearing on their social status, are discussed below.

The marital status of the aged people greatly influences their life style. Losing the spouse in old age brings a very hard time in the passage of one's life and the living partner has to face all the problems of old age with rarely someone to share with or understand.

Table 1 shows the age and marital status of 380 aged men and women. There is a predominance of married men (35.26%) and widows (26.31%) over married women (22.89%) and widowers (13.94%) in all the age groups. In an Angami society, it is the moral responsibility for every individual to get married. But it has been found that 0.52 per cent of the aged women remain single. This is possibly because they did not get a suitable or desirable partner or they decided to remain single and look after their aged parents. At the same time there are more widows than widowers

TABLE 1: Age and Marital Status of the Aged

Age Groups	SIngle		Married		Widower/ Widow		Divorced		Total	%
	Men	Women	Men	Women	Men	Women	Men	Women		
60-65	1	2	46	35	7	28	1	1	121	31.84
65-70	-	-	31	24	13	25	1	-	94	24.73
70-75	-	-	18	10	10	20	-	-	58	15.26
75-80	-	-	18	14	8	11	-	-	51	13.42
80+	-	-	21	4	15	16	-	-	56	14.73
Total	1	2	134	87	53	100	2	1	380	100
%	0.26	0.52	35.26	22.89	13.94	26.31	0.52	0.26	100	

Source: Field Work.

Table 2: Educational Level of the Aged

Educational Level	Men		Women	
	Number	Percentage	Number	Percentage
Illiterate	95	50	95	50
Literate with no formal education	2	1.05	2	1.05
Primary to High School	50	26.31	72	37.89
High School to Intermediate	31	16.31	19	10
Graduate and Postgraduate	8	4.21	2	1.05
Technical Education	4	2.1	Nil	-
Total	190	100	190	100

Source: Field Work.

because remarriage of widows is prohibited whereas widowers, remarriage takes place under certain conditions. Another reason could be a higher mortality rate of man due to hard work or they did not take care of their health properly. An interesting comparison is afforded by a study conducted by Bond et al. in California (1954), where too, there are more married men than women are and more widows than widowers are. It also shows that unmarried women (0.52%) are more than men (0.26%) are. It may further be noted that there are no divorcees or separatees above the age of 65 nor are there any bachelors or spinsters above this age. There is a sharp decline in the percentage of the aged in the age group of 75 to 80.

In modern times education is one of the important determinants of a person's social status. It is one of the most important factors responsible for helping a person to move up the social ladder. A study of the educational accomplishments of the Angami aged shows that 48.94 per cent of the women respondents received formal education as against 46.83 per cent in the case of men. 2.10 per cent of the aged men respondents received technical education, but there is no case of technical graduate among the women respondents (Table 2). Majority of the aged population received education from primary to below high school (64.2%); only 4.21 per cent of the aged men received graduate and postgraduate degrees as against 1.05 per cent in the case of women. When asked why they did not go for higher studies, the reply was that as soon as they passed matriculation they opted for job, which was easy to get those days, and some started doing business. 1.05 per cent of the aged are found to be literate without any formal education.

In an Angami family, normally the father is the chief bread earner of the family, but in some cases if the husband is unemployed and wife is employed then she becomes the chief bread earner of the family. The study revealed that 48.68 per cent of the Angami aged respondents were still the chief bread earners of their families (Table 3). About 20 per cent of the respondents were economically dependent and 31.31 per cent were partially dependent. Among the women, 31.57 per cent respondents were the chief bread earners of the families as against 65.78 per cent in the case of men. 28.42 per cent of women were wholly dependent upon others and 40 per cent partially dependent, whereas 11.57 per cent of aged men were wholly dependent upon others and 22.63 per cent were partially dependent. Thus, dependency among the women was more pronounced than among the men respondents. But the burden of the aged in supporting their children's education is still very high.

The study shows that all the respondents are staying in their own houses. This is in fact very natural thing to notice in Nagaland. Even if it is a mud hut or a very humble house every married man has to have a house of his own unless he is living in the ancestral house. One cannot simply imagine anyone with a family and not having a house of his own, particularly in the rural areas. Even in the urban areas of Nagaland, not to have a house of one's own, particularly for the Nagas, is something rare, if not impossible. Thus, present study indicates that 100 per cent of the respondents live in their own houses. However, it does not really say much about their other socio-economic characteristics.

The Angamis prefer to stay with their aged parents even after marriage. A family seldom exceeds five members. So they are easily adjusted in a household (Hutton 1962:55). The study on the living arrangement of the aged shows that as many as 75.78 per cent of the aged live with their children and only 8.64 per cent of them live alone. 14.21 per cent of the aged respondents are living with their spouses and only 1.31

Table 3: Status of the Aged in Family According to Sex

Status in the Family	Men		Women		Total	
	Number	%	Number	%	Number	%
Chief Bread-earners	125	65.78	60	31.57	185	48.68
Wholly Dependent	22	11.57	54	28.42	76	20
Partially Dependent	43	22.63	76	40	119	31.31
Total	190	100	190	100	380	100
Percentage	50		50			

Source: Field Work.

per cent are living with their married daughters or sons-in-law (Table 4).

All the aged respondents living alone earn their own livelihood. 14.21 per cent respondents live with their spouses among whom majority of the men were the chief bread earners while majority of the women were dependent (Table 4). 75.78 per cent of the respondents live with their children, 30.78 per cent are chief bread earners, 27.36 per cent are partially dependent and 17.63 per cent are wholly dependent on their children. Among the aged more men than women are chief bread earners. Of the 1.31 per cent living with married daughters- or sons-in-law, none of them is the chief bread earner, 0.52 per cent is partially dependent and 0.78 per cent is wholly dependent. 10 per cent of the aged are staying alone because either their wife or husband had died or they did not have any children or all their children are married. And after the death of their spouse, they had chosen to stay alone rather than choosing to stay with their married children.

75.78 per cent of the aged respondents are staying with their children because they prefer to stay with them and it is also considered the responsibility of their children to look after them in old age. 1.31 per cent of the aged are compelled to stay with their sons-in-law (Table 4) because they do not have any son and after the marriage of their daughters they live along with their daughters.

In the higher age groups of the aged respondents, the proportion of those living with their children decreased progressively. There can be two possible explanations for this. One, their children got married or they had no children at all. The other could be that the aged started earning their own living and preferred to live with their own spouses rather than moving into the families of their children as dependents.

Owing to the high level of unemployment among the working-age-group population, employment of the aged is relegated to the background. The occupational status and degree of economic security enjoyed by an individual in old age seems to have some influence on their attitude towards aging. A study on the occupation of the Angamis shows that, out of 380 respondents, 235 (103 men and 132 women), i.e., 61.84 per cent are cultivators (Table 5). 14.47 per cent are retired government servants, 3.68 are working as manual labourers/quarry workers, 11.05 per cent are church/social workers and only 5.52 per cent are doing some business.

Thus, most of the aged are cultivators and their chief source of livelihood is agriculture. The second highest group among the aged belongs to those who have retired from government service. The aged Angamis are also involved in church and other social activities. 5.52 per cent of the aged are doing business. Only 3.68 per cent are working as manual or quarry workers (Table 5). This is probably because it is the only source of income for them to maintain their family.

B. Economic Status of the Aged

In general, old age is accompanied by a decline in economic status and the aged tend to have low income and little accumulated wealth. As a result, many of them are not in a position to maintain even the minimum standards of food, clothing, housing and social amenities. However, neither all the aged respondents are living in the same economic condition nor are they adversely affected in the same way or to the same extent. The variation in economic conditions seems to mainly depend upon the status and nature of occupation as well as on the sex and marital status of the person, his/her health, social obligations and control over economic resources.

In Angami society, income is not the sole determinant of a person's economic status. For an

TABLE 4: Living Arrangement of the Aged According to Age And Sex

	AGE-GROUPS											
	60-65		65-70		70-75		75-80		80+			
	M	W	M	W	M	W	M	W	M	W	Total	%
Living Alone CBE	3	7	2	4	5	6	1	2	2	1	33 (8.64)	8.64
PD												
WD												
Living with Spouse CBE	10		8	3	3	2	4	3	2		35 (9.21)	
PD	1	1		4	1	3				3	13 (3.42)	14.21
WD	1	1		2		1				1	6 (1.57)	
Living with children CBE	32	14	26	9	12	4	8	5	4	3	117 (30.78)	
PD	6	25	5	19	7	10	9	6	10	7	104 (27.36)	75.78
WD	2	18	4	8		4	4	9	13	5	67 (17.63)	

(*contd.*)

AGE-GROUPS

	60-65		65-70		70-75		75-80		80+			
	M	W	M	W	M	W	M	W	M	W	Total	%
CBE												
Living with												
married PD									2		2	
daughter											(0.52)	
(S-I-L)									3		3	1.31
WD											(0.52)	
Men	55		45		28		26		36		190	100
Women	66		49		30		25		20		190	
Total	121		94		58		51		56		380	

Source: Fieldwork

Index: CBE = chief bread earner
PD = partially dependent
WD = wholly dependent
S-I-L = sons-in-law
M = men
W = women

Table 5: Occupation of the Aged

Occupation	Men		Women		Total	%
	Number	Percentage	Number	Percentage		
Retired Govt. Servants	41	21.57	14	7.36	55	14.47
Manual labourers/ Quarry workers	5	2.63	9	4.73	14	3.68
Cultivators	103	54.21	132	69.47	235	61.84
Church/ Social workers	20	10.52	22	11.57	42	11.05
Business	16	8.42	5	2.63	21	5.52
Bedridden	5	2.63	8	4.21	13	3.42
Total	190	100	190	100	380	100

Source: Field Work

Angami a person is considered rich, if he/she is self-sufficient and has enough rice bunds ***(Chünuo)*** for daily consumption. Because of this, even though the Angamis still practise the indigenous methods of cultivation, every family works hard to get the required rice bunds. Thus, if a person cannot produce enough rice for the family for one year then he/she is considered poor. At the same time, the number of cows and land a person owns is also taken into account for considering a person rich or poor. Thus, in traditional Angami society, if a person has accumulated a harvest of 10-20 years rice bunds then a "feast of merit" is given. Normally, 5-10 rice bunds and 10-15 cows are needed to give a feast of merit depending on the size of the village. In fact through this the rich people gain more social status and at the same time come down to the level of the common people and start earning for the next feast. It is because of this that there is less disparity between the rich and the poor in traditional Angami society.

Through modernization, the Angami society is also changing but the economic status is still measured as before though money power seems to be taking the upper hand in Angami society.

Economic status of the Angami aged has been assessed from their income and assets such as house, land and the number of rice bunds and cows.

Income and occupation are, among others, two very important and closely related determinants of status. The Angamis in general are likely to have better income than the other communities because they have better avenues of livelihood since the state capital Kohima is in their land. The present study on the Angami aged reveals that 93.69 per cent of the aged have some income of their own. The remaining 6.31 per cent have no source of income. 53.42 per cent of the aged are in the low-income group (Table 6) with monthly income less than Rs. 1,000. 33.68 per cent are in the category

Table 6: Income of the Aged

INCOME GROUP	INCOME	No. of Cases	Percentage	Total (%)
Lower Income Group 1-1000 (Rs)	No Income	24	6.31	203 (53.42)
	Upto 200	62	16.31	
	201-400	16	4.21	
	401-600	40	10.52	
	601-800	15	3.94	
	801-1000	46	12.10	
Middle Income Group 1001-6000 (Rs)	1001-2000	47	12.36	128 (33.68)
	2001-3000	38	10	
	3001-4000	12	3.15	
	4001-5000	24	6.31	
	5001-6000	7	1.84	
Upper Income Group 6001+ (Rs)	6001-7000	15	3.94	49 (12.89)
	7001-8000	3	0.78	
	8001-9000	10	2.63	
	9001-10000	12	3.15	
	10,000+	9	2.36	
Total		380	100	380(100)

Source: Field Work.

of middle income group, having income less than Rs. 6,000 and 12.89 per cent (Table 6) are in the upper income group.

The aged having no income have to depend upon their children to fulfil their daily necessities. They often have to face economic and psychological tensions in the family due to this dependent status. As aged parents, they too have certain social obligations like attending marriages, deaths of their kins, and so on. All this involves substantial expenditure on their part. Without any income or with low income it is very difficult for the aged parents to meet these social obligations and they feel hesitant to ask for financial help from their children.

Thus, the study reveals that as far as income of the Angami aged is concerned almost all have some income of their own but the same is too meagre to maintain their family. The economic status of the Angami aged can be further understood by analyzing the number of rice bunds and cows a person owns.

Of those with some earning, 3.93 per cent have income from wages, 15.16 from self-employment, 19.10 from property/house rent, 2.80 from interest on saving, 16.31 from pension which include 10.95 and 8.4:2 from government pension and old age pension respectively. 23.59 per cent earn from selling of farm products and 16.01 have more than one source of income (Table 7). For most aged Angamis the only source of income is from selling of farm products, self-employment and property or house rent. Interest in saving forms the lowest source of income of the aged, which is followed by salary and wages. Old age pension is the third lowest source of income of the aged, which is not at all adequate.

As an individual grows old his/her physical and mental strength gradually decreases. Consequently,

Table 7: Sources of Income of the Aged According to Income Group (Earners Only)

Source of Income	Income Group				
	Lower Income Group	Middle Income Group	Upper Income Group	Total	Percentage
Wages	9	3	2	14	3.93
Self employed	29	20	5	54	15.16
Property/House Rent	30	28	10	68	19.1
Interest on Saving	9	1	-	10	2.8
Pensions Govt. Employee pension	12	18	9	39	10.95
Old age Pension	8	17	5	30	8.42
Selling of Farm Products	51	17	16	84	23.59
More than one source of income	20	27	10	57	16.01
Total	168	131	57	356	100
Percentage	47.19	36.79	16.01	100	

Source: Field Work.

they are not being able to perform certain roles and works, which they were previously performing.

Table 8 indicates that in the age group of 60 to 65, 98.34 per cent of the aged have some kind of income and only 1.65 per cent has no income. Again in the age group of 65 to 70, 98.93 per cent aged have income and 1.06 per cent respondents are without any income, and in 70 to 75 years group, 91.37 per cent have income and 8.62 per cent have no income. In the two higher age groups, i.e., 75-80 and 80+, the aged having income are 88.23 and 82.14 per cent respectively and those without income are 11.76 and 17.85 per cent respectively. So, the study reveals that as the age increases, the number of aged with income decreases. Thus, as the aged becomes older their earning capacity decreases and they become dependent on their children.

Table 8: Earning Capacity According to Age Groups

Age Groups	With Income	Without Income	Total	%age
60 - 65	119 (98.34)	2 (1.65)	121	31.84
65 - 70	93 (98.93)	1 (1.06)	94	24.73
70 - 75	53 (91.37)	5 (8.62)	58	15.26
75 - 80	45 (88.23)	6 (11.76)	51	13.42
80+	46 (82.14)	10 (17.85)	56	14.73
Total	356	24	380	100
Percentage	93.68	6.32	100	

Source: Field Work.
Note: Figures in parentheses are in percentages.

Table 9 shows the old age pension beneficiaries in Nagaland, Kohima district and in the study area.

The study reveals that out of 63,777 aged population in Nagaland (Census 1991) 11,194 (17.55%) are getting Old Age Pensions. In Kohima district, 11.60 per cent are availing old age pensions whereas only 4.98 per

Table 9: Beneficiaries of Old Age Assistance

Old age Assistance	Nagaland		Kohima District		Study area	
	No. of aged 60+	Beneficiaries	No. of aged 60+	Beneficiaries	No. of aged 60+	Beneficiaries
Old Age Pension (70+)		8794	14,138	1206	1023	39
National Old Age Pension (65+)	63, 777	2400		435		12
Total	63,777	11,194	14,138	1641	1023	51
Percentage		17.55		11.6		4.98

cent of the aged in the study area are enjoying such pensions.

Since the aged people have become weak and the earning capacity is low, most of them fall in the lower income group and as such old age assistance is an important source of income for them. But the study shows that only 4.98 per cent of the aged respondents in the study area are getting old age pension. This shows that many needy aged persons in the study area are not getting it because 165 (43.42%) of the aged are above the age of 70. And any elderly persons crossing the age of 70 years are entitled to get old age pension. Some possible reasons for not availing the same are: (1) they are not aware of old age assistance, (2) their children are taking care of them, and (3) they have applied but did not get.

A description of the economic status of the families of the Angami aged can reveal the extent to which these families are able to look after the aged. The discussion on the economic status of such families includes all the aged whether they are chief bread-earners or are partially or wholly dependent.

Table 10 shows that 51.57 per cent of the families belong to the Low Income Group, 28.42 per cent to Middle Income Group, and 22.63 per cent to the Upper Income Group. Of these 6.31 per cent of the families have no income. On the other hand, 2.36 per cent of the families have income above Rs.10,000 per month.

Table 10: Income of the Families of the Aged

Income Group	No. of Families	Percentage
Low Income Group	196	51.57
Middle Income Group	108	28.42
Upper Income Group	86	22.63
Total	380	100.00

Source: Field Work..

These figures show that about half of the aged respondents live with families whose economic position is very low. Only one-fifth of the families are in the upper income group. This is further demonstrated by the number of persons in the family as shown in Table 11.

Table 11: Average Size of the Family by Economic Status

Income Group	No. of Families	No. of Family Members	Average Size of the Family
Lower Income Group	179	878	4.90
Middle Income Group	114	503	4.41
Upper Income Group	87	371	4.26
Total	380	1752	4.61

Source: Fieldwork

Table 11 shows that there are 1752 persons in the 380 families in which the aged live, the average size of the family working out to 4.61 per family, but varying from 4.90 in families belonging to the Lower Income Group to 4.26 in families belonging to the Higher Income Group. From this it can be seen that the families in the Lower Income Group have more dependents than in the Higher Income Group or the Middle Income Group. So, not only is their economic status lower but they also have more family members to be fed, educated, and clothed. Out of 380 families, 179 (47.10%) of the families fall under the category of Lower Income Group.

Another important aspect that seems to influence the economic status of the aged people is their assets and liabilities. Among the Angamis, four items of assets, which have a bearing on their economic status, are discussed here. They are house/building, land, rice bund and cow the aged own at the time of enquiry. The maintenance of the family, including education and marriage of their children are taken here as liabilities, which are yet to be met by the aged.

Immovable property can be in the form of houses and land and consumable assets like rice and cows. Table 12 reveals that 58.42 per cent of the aged have houses for their own use and 41.57 per cent have houses for rent also. So, from their assets also they get some money for their maintenance. 76.84 per cent of the aged in lower income group own only one house, 23.15 per cent have at least two houses, of which one is for rental. In the middle and upper income groups, 59.37 and 71.42 per cent of the aged have houses, both for their use and rental respectively. This shows that the aged in these income groups have more sources of income and as such their economic status is also higher than that of other income groups.

Another important asset of the aged is land, which is either irrigated or non-irrigated. In all the income groups most of the aged respondents have both irrigated and non-irrigated lands. Twenty per cent of them have irrigated and 16.57 per cent have non-irrigated land and 63.42 per cent have both irrigated and non-irrigated land (Table 12). Though the aged people do not have much source of income they have enough land to cultivate rice, vegetables, etc. for their daily consumption.

A rice bund is a giant basket made of bamboo strips, which is used for storing paddy. Its size ranges from 3 to 4 feet in diameter and 7 to 8 feet in height and can hold about 400- 500 kilograms of paddy. It is an important determinant of economic status of the Angamis. The prestige and economic status of a person is assessed on the basis of the rice bunds, which are stored for 10-20 years or more depending upon the family. The average family size is found to be 4.61 per family and as such two rice bunds are sufficient for the whole family for one year. Depending on this it has been

Table 12: Assets of the Aged

Income Group	House		Land			Rice bunds		No. of Families having Cow
	Own use	Rental	Irrigated	Non-irrigated	Both	Less than 2	2 or more than 2	
Lower Income Group	156 (76.84)	47 (23.15)	51 (25.12)	42 (20.68)	110 (54.18)	56 (27.58)	147 (72.41)	49 (24.13)
Middle Income Group	52 (40.62)	76 (59.37)	18 (14.06)	16 (12.50)	94 (73.43)	39 (30.46)	89 (69.53)	33 (25.78)
Upper Income Group	14 (28.57)	35 (71.42)	7 (14.28)	5 (10.20)	37 (75.51)	8 (16.32)	41 (83.67)	16 (32.65)
Total	222 (58.42)	158 (41.57)	76 (20.00)	63 (16.57)	241 (63.42)	103 (27.10)	277 (72.89)	98 (25.78)

Source: Field Work.
Note: Figures in parentheses are in percentages.

classified into two categories, family having less than two rice bunds and those having two or more than two rice bunds. In the Angami society, self-sufficiency is one of the key values and for this they work hard to achieve it. Surplus production and selling of rice is hardly known. The study reveals that 27.10 per cent of the aged have less than two rice bunds and 72.89 per cent have two or more than two rice bunds. This shows that about three-fourth of the Angami aged respondents are self-sufficient in terms of food availability, which is one of their top priorities.

In the traditional Angami culture, the number of cows a person owns also plays an important role in determining the economic status of the aged in the society. Feast of Merit is usually performed to gain prestige and economic status. During this feast 5-10 cows were slaughtered for the party but it is no longer observed and as such many families have stopped rearing cows. The study on the number of families having cows reveals that only 25.78 per cent of the Angami aged own cows, which still a determinant of economic status in the society.

Thus the study on the economic status of the Angami aged shows that, though 53.42 per cent of the aged have income less than Rs.1,000 per month, 63.42 per cent of the aged have enough land to cultivate vegetables, rice etc. At the same time 72.89 per cent of the aged are found to be self-sufficient with two or more than two rice bunds which is enough for the family to survive even if there is a natural calamity. So in terms of income, the Angami aged are economically poor but when it comes to rice-bunds, which is the most important characteristic in determining the economic status, they are self-sufficient.

Liabilities are a major problem faced by the aged. It can be in the form of family maintenance, education, and marriage of their children and grandchildren. Table

Table 13: Liabilities of the Aged

Income Group	Liabilities for the Children/Grandchildren			Family Maintenance
	Children's education	Grandchildren's education	Children's marriage	
Lower Income Group	38 (18.71)	5 (2.46)	71 (34.97)	89 (43.84)
Middle Income Group	35 (27.34)	7 (5.46)	45 (35.15)	41 (32.03)
Upper Income Group	17 (34.69)	2 (4.08)	21 (42.85)	9 (18.36)
Total	90 (23.68)	14 (3.68)	137 (36.05)	139 (36.57)

Source: Field Work.
Note: Figures in parentheses are in percentages.

13 shows that majority of the aged respondents have liabilities towards education and marriage of their children and grandchildren. One hundred thirty-nine respondents (36.5%) have liabilities towards their family maintenance. In the lower income group, 18.71 per cent of the aged have liabilities towards their children's education, 2.46 per cent towards their grandchildren's education, 34.97 per cent towards their marriage, and 43.84 per cent towards family maintenance. In the middle and upper income groups, liabilities towards children's marriage are more than towards their education. Liabilities for children's marriage are the highest (35.15%) in the upper income group. Though maximum of the respondents are in the middle and upper income groups, liabilities for their children and grandchildren towards their education and marriage are also more. In all the three income groups, the aged respondents have liabilities towards their grandchildren as well. This is because, in some cases, the aged persons want to help their sons by looking after at least one of their children but in some cases, their parents were divorced and so the parents looked after their children.

Conclusion

The study on the Angami aged shows that most aged people enjoy married life and there are more married men than women and more widows than widowers. At the same time, there are more unmarried women than such men. Education is an important determinant of a person's social status. In an Angami society, illiteracy is more pronounced among the aged women than among such men. But among the literate respondents, formal education is more significant among the women than men. None of the aged women has gone for technical education. Most aged respondents have received education from primary to high school level and only a few of them have studied upto graduation or post graduation.

In a nuclear family, birth of a son is a security of the aged people and perhaps because of this most of the Angami aged respondents' stay with their married sons. It is interesting to know that all the aged respondents live in houses owned by themselves. Some of them are staying with their spouses and their children. Of those who are staying with their children in the same household, majority are still the chief bread-earners of the families.

About half of the aged people are chief bread-earners of their families. One-fifth of the aged respondents are wholly dependent upon others and the rest are partially dependent. Dependency among the women is more pronounced than among the men due to lack of education or employment. Thus, the burden of the aged women in supporting their children is higher than that of aged men.

Some of the aged Angamis are compelled to stay with their in-laws, because they do not have any son or all their daughters are married. Of those who are staying with their in- laws, they are either partially or wholly dependent. But in all other cases, whether the aged are staying alone or with spouses or with children, the aged are by and large the chief bread earners of the family.

Most of the Angami aged respondents are cultivators and they continue with their daily works to maintain their families. Aged respondents doing business is negligible. Only a few of the aged people are retired government servants. Many of them are involved in social and church activities.

Economic position is an important determinant of social status. The study reveals that most of the aged have income of their own. But half of the aged having income of their own fall under the category of lower income group. Thus, though they have income of their own, it is not sufficient to manage their families by that alone. It is significant that about half of the aged draw their income from selling of farm products, and property/house rent and a few from government pensions and old age assistance. Income from salary and wages and interest on saving is very meagre. The study reveals that with increasing age, the earning capacity decreases and the aged people become dependent on their children.

Looking at the economic status of the families in which the aged people in Angami society live, it appears that most of such families are in the lower income group. At the same time, the families in the lower income group have more dependents than in the higher income groups. Thus, as far as income is concerned their economic status is low and also they have more family members to look after.

An analysis of the assets and liabilities of the aged shows that most aged Angamis still have to fulfill their major responsibilities connected with the education and marriage of their children. The aged respondents in the lower income group have in particular more liabilities than the aged people in the middle or upper income groups. In terms of assets, all the aged respondents have a house of their own. 41.57 per cent of the aged have two or three houses and most of them fall in the category of middle and upper income groups. The Angami aged are found to be self-sufficient because the study reveals that 72.89 per cent of the aged have two or more than two rice bunds, which is enough for an average family to survive for one year.

Thus, the aged Angamis in the lower income group have less source income but more liabilities, which make them both poorer and dependent than the Angamis belonging to the other income groups. Though maximum of the aged are in the lower income group, all the aged have enough irrigated or non-irrigated land at their disposal, where they can cultivate rice, vegetables etc. and supplement their income. Self-sufficiency, which is the top priority of the Angamis, is found quite common among of the aged.

Self-will is the Strongest will for Elderly Persons

REFERENCES

Bhatia, H.S. (1983), *Aging and Societies,* Udaipur: Arya's Book Centre.

Birren, J. and V. Clayton (1975), *History of Gerentology,* New York: D.Van Nostrand Co.

Bond, Floyd A. *et al. Our Needy Aged: A California Study of the National Problem,* New York: Henry Holt and Co.

Census of India (1991), *Ageing Population of India: An analysis of the 1991 Census,* New Delhi: Registrar General of Census Operation.

Channa, S.M. (1992), *Nagaland - A Contemporary Ethnography,* New Delhi: Cosmo Publications.

Dutt, R. (1986), *Social Institution in India,* Bombay: Tata Institute of Social Sciences.

Hurlock, J. (1983), *Problems of Aging,* California: Dickenson Publishing Company.

Hutton, J.H. (1963), *The Angami Nagas,* Bombay: Oxford University Press.

6

THE NEED FOR ESTABLISHMENT OF OLD AGED HOME, PEOPLE SUPPORT AND PROSPECT AND SCOPE IN NAGA SOCIETY

—I. Tongdangba Jamir

In many foreign countries including some cities in India there are many old age homes, managed by Governments, Societies and NGO's etc. and many old peoples stay there and spend the rest of their life.

In case of Nagaland, there is no such institution or Old age home at present and the Old Aged people are looked after by the family members or relatives only. The traditional system of keeping elderly persons in Naga society is not very much satisfactory, providing daily food and shelter are not enough but they require both physical and mental satisfaction for their longevity of life. Moreover, the traditional system has weakened slowly due to the following reasons such as mass immigration of youngsters to the urban areas leaving the old people to feed themselves, increase in cost of living, and disintegration of society and family norms. More and more women are taking active part in working sectors (Government or private services) and they cannot spare much time to take care of the elderly with the family. However, the existing traditions can still be strengthened through the help and support by NGO's, societies and churches, visiting them regularly and encouraging the family members and also supporting and counseling the elderly persons for peaceful life.

Earlier, in Ao villages, there were SEMTU in every *khel,* where the sentries spent the day guarding the village. There, the old people of the *khel* who could not go to field or work gathered and spent the days sharing their problems and for those who were gifted persons, used to made baskets, mats, cane chairs, utensils and wood crafts etc. Thus, they spent the days happily, busily engaged in various. The youngsters may consider to revive such activities with additional one inclusive of women also to spend their precious lifetime happily.

The **International Day for Elderly—**1st October of every year was designated as the International day for the elderly by UNO and is being celebrated all over the world. For the first time on 1st October 1999, the International Day for Elderly was celebrated here at Mokokchung also sponsored by the District Pensioner's Association with great joy. Many prominent Senior Citizens in Mokokchung town attended the function and actively participated in discussion. The participants identified the following main problems of the old people such boredom, feeling worthlessness, loneliness, lack of health care etc. The members were convinced that establishment of a Day Care Centre for the Elderly was of more pressing needs than the Old Age Home in the present situation and decided to establish a Day Care Centre for the Elderly with the following aims and objectives:

1. To create people's awareness about the problems and suffering of old age.
2. To create avenue to spend the days together with their friends sharing their problems, experiences and recollecting their youthful life,

3. To offer opportunities to share knowledge and experiences by arranging Seminars, functions etc. on the topics of interest and beneficial to them,

4. To arrange and conduct regular health check up and cares, with facilities not easily available in their hand, and

5. To arrange and conduct counseling, retreat and prayer meetings etc.

The project is the first of its kind in Nagaland and in the history of the Elderly in the state of Nagaland. It is now functioning very effectively gathering the needs of the Elderly in the district particularly in Mokokchung town. It is one step forward towards welfare activities for sufferings of the Old Aged people. The building costing nearly Rs.15,00,000 lakh have been completed with donations from public, pensioners and grant from Government. The Site located in the centre area of Mokokchung Town was donated by Dr & Mrs. Senkalong Yaden and the project programs are yet to be taken up as early as possible. We pray that, let this can be an eye-opener for all NGO's, Societies, youngsters and the churches, who are having concern for the welfare of the Old Aged People to lend their helping hands.

Nagaland Pensioners' Association

The Nagaland Pensioners' Association is a well organized Association registered under Registration of Societies Act of 1960. It is affiliated with the Bharat Pensioners' Samaj, New Delhi (a member in International Federation on Ageing, Montreal, Canada). There are District Pensioners' Association in all the districts in Nagaland, affiliated with the Nagaland Pensioners' Association. Its main objectives are to look after the welfare of the pensioners and the family pensioners including elderly people. They have a well defined working by-laws aiming effective management fulfilling its objects. Mokokchung District Pensioners' Association was formed on 11th November, 1981.

After its establishment—many problems of the pensioners faced earlier for drawal of monthly pension have been solved with the treasuries and Bank branches and there is no such serious problem at least in the case of Mokokchung district Pensioners' for drawing pension.

According to Central Service Pension Rules, 1972, sub rule 64 the Pension Payment Order (PPO) should be issued one month before the retirement of the government servant or immediately after retirement and the provisional pension payment should be arranged by the 1st day of every month.

The above instruction or rules given in the Pension Rules, 1972 are never carried out by the government department or by Accountant General and thus the government employees on retirement are put into much financial hardships which can be avoided if the above pension rules are carried out seriously.

Regarding difficulties from the Accountant General Office in settlement of Pension and Family pension cases, it is always delayed causing untold financial hardships to the pensioners and their families. Besides, they have to spend huge amount of money seeking to get their pension cases settled, roaming from office to office.

The following remedial measures are suggested:

1. The Government departments should process the pension cases of the retiring employees in time as per Central Civil Service Pension Rules.
2. The Accountant General on receipt of the pension papers should immediately arrange to

check and rectify or get it rectified in case of any defect or mistakes.

3. The State Government should consider for opening a separate Pension Directorate Cell specially to deal with the Pensioners and Family Pensioners.

4. Lastly, it is suggested that for the Elderly People, the state Government should consider for issuing Senior Citizen Certificate to enable them to avail concession and facilities in the country.

Never Discourage. Be Strong and Courageous,
We are Here to Take Care of You.

7

THE AGED PEOPLE IN DIMAPUR: PROBLEMS AND PROSPECTS

—Mar Atsongchanger

Introduction

Many of you might have celebrated your birthdays in the last six months, and this tells us that we are getting a lot older. To make us look younger we can buy numerous anti-ageing products—face creams, hair dyes and toning creams. But these do not stop growing us older. This process of ageing will happen to us until finally we die. Every wrinkle and every gray hair is God's wake-up call to us and it reminds us that we would not last forever in our present age. Life begins at birth but the life of a responsible person may begin at different age, while some are married at 20s some may marry at 50s and as a result, even the ageing may differ from person to person. Therefore, irrespective of strength or responsibilities either family or in society, the United Nations agreed that the cut-off age above 60 years to refer as 'older population'.

In traditional Naga society one of the qualifications to act as a representative of the society in all matters of difficulty and deliberation is 'old people'. Although there is no bar to be categorized as old, as per the government service rule, anyone who attains the retirement from active govt. service can be grouped as 'old people'. Yet in a society where longevity extends up to 80 years we may consider an aged who is over 80 above.

When is a person old?

Ageing may differ from culture to culture. Because retirement varies, can be early or late. While some retired by age others may be retired by years of service. Therefore retirement cannot be a measuring age, yet it can qualify one for the title of 'senior citizen'. According to Hebrew Society, the age at which one was considered as 'qualified' was apparently at sixty (Leviticus 27: 1-8). Those over sixty years paid a significantly reduced temple tax, which was an indication that sixty was a semiofficial retirement age in Israel. *(Gilmore,* 1992:2) While even among them the Levite priests had an earlier retirement, they were to quit the office at fifty (Numbers 8:24-26), with the option of being part-time. In contrast to the Hebrew society, in the Ao Naga society, while the age is important, anyone who are in the Putu *Menden* are consider as an elder, which implies old. Therefore in a strict sense, to define who is old is a matter to decide in certain cases.

Dimapur Case Studies

The city of Dimapur can be rightly called as the Commercial Capital of Nagaland. It has an easy accessible with airplane and Indian Railways making itself an easy transit for everyone for entering to mainland India. In terms of social dominant unlike other towns in Nagaland, Dimapur is a place where nobody is under any tribe/race, paving its freedom for own style of living. However, with this freedom, one will also find that, the traditional bonds of the Naga society are slowly diminishing in this city. In order to get a comprehensive views from a wider spectrum, out of twenty interviewed on random sampling with the retired person from different walks of life, taking into consideration on economics status but only a few views are given below.

1. Mr. Rongsenmeren Longchar (b.1940)

Born in Waromong Village. He was retired on 2002 and his wife on 2006 after 24 and 35 years of government service respectively. Upon the inquiry he has few comments for coming to Dimapur:

(a) He has narrated the story how he purchased his land in Dimapur, that without any pre-plan but rather a sudden decision. Therefore, to him the retirement life to be at Dimapur was not a pleasant choice but a compulsion from the children.

(b) The other disadvantage he feels at Dimapur is 'in Dimapur there is no "*Sungkum*" or 'Village gate' which means no social rules or norms. In case of a dead there is nobody to dig the ground for burial, one has to pay for the last rites. Otherwise, it should be done with all the dignity and honor. He says it's a curse for the Naga society.

(c) There is no home visitation because each known friend is far away from the other. Lack of giving '*aon*' to the next door. Recalling a warm fellowship in the traditional Naga set-up; usually in any Naga society the neighbors set together to share joys and sorrows, share any food items when it is still hot, but those cultures are completely lost in Dimapur.

(d) On the whole he has his advantage of coming to Dimapur are, the climatic conditions and the plain geographical locations that are favorable for the old age.

2. Mr. N. Imti Ao, NCS, Jt. Secretary (Retd.) (b.1941)

Imti Ao served for 38 years under Govt. of Nagaland. Started his career as Secretariat staff and later became a Civil Servant through Nagaland Public Service Commission. Served in various capacities before full retirement in 1998. His last Home as Dimapur was not a choice, he was born in Mokokchung and planned, to settled in Mokokchung but situation compelled him for final home to be constructed in Dimapur. Following his settlement in Dimapur has various experience and few are stated below:

(a) Dimapur provides him many 'challenging avenues even after the retirement. He enrolled in Nagaland Bar Association and started practicing Law. His advocacy works are more on humanitarian services rather than fees work. Therefore, with no fee/nominal fees he helps many poor people.

(b) With four Aged Persons, formed a band 'Gospel Melody' in 1998. This band helps him to develop a closer fellowship not only among the four members but also with larger group through different participation; church, singing, social gathering and villager's fellowships.

(c) By being at Dimapur it was an opportunity for him to serve in social forums. He served in Dimapur Naga Council as General Secretary 2000-2004. Such association among all the Nagas in Dimapur enables him to extend the social boundary with wider circle. All these activities keep him busy at all the time.

(d) The disappointment in Dimapur for him is the prevalence of anti-social activities. This trend is becoming more and more, making unsafe for the weak and old people. As such the movements are restricted with these practices, the freedom of minds are also restricted.

(e) On the question of opening an Aged Home, he opines that, Nagas are traditionally self-dependent even at the ripe age. If an old person/parents are put into such Home by the children, the society may not approve or may be a social stigma on the part of old/aged person as well. But instead an Aged Recreational Home may be useful, where all the aged can come and play, share, sing, chat or listen to one another. Share the memories, ideas and learn from each other.

(f) Experiencing from his old age association and also as he involved with the Dimapur District Ao Pensioners Union as its Secretary since January 2006 he has highlighted a few programs initiated by the Pensioners for the old people such as;

- Organized a fellowship once in every three months (Get together)
- Arranged seminars on health, forestry, fisheries etc.
- In every funeral of a member Rs.500 are given as token of love.

3. Rev. A Temjen (b.1922)

Rev. A. Temjen was born in a small village called Dibuia, under Mokokchung District. Did his early education from Impur and later did his theological studies at Jorhat. He started his ministry as a Teacher in Alongkima middle school, but his service was required at Mission Hqs. Impur and worked there till his retirement in 1988. He chose his home to be at Dimapur and resides here happily since then.

(a) He stays alone with mixture of feelings, he has concerns for many social issues at this ripe age, and one of his concerns is; Dimapur is a cosmopolitan city with inter-tribal (between the various Nagas) marriages or inter-cultural marriages. Therefore if each tribe/cultural identities are to maintain without acknowledging each other, it will bring shame within the families of inter/mixed marriages. A situational example as, if a driver runs-over a chick, he quickly imposed a fine and he has to pay the fine without raising any voice. But such random actions reflect on the mixed marriages families resulting disharmony between the spouses. His aim at this age is to propagate a common culture that is acceptable to all.

(b) To the question on the problems of the aged facing today in the children's house he sensed that many of the aged are becoming unwanted, specially when there are visitors or any important meetings in their houses. There are also certain cases, when they are kept under the room whole day. He subscribes for an Aged Home at Dimapur.

(c) With geographical distances another problem has been added for the aged, they are unable to meet their childhood friends although they are in the same city. Unless somebody takes them with proper appointment there is no chance to see each other. This is a contrast culture from the traditional social setup.

(d) As a writer he finds more time in Dimapur. Idea collections and putting them into papers occupies his time and therefore he enjoys his old age days in Dimapur. He also testifies that, his lonesome moments are the best time to have fellowship with his Lord.

4. Er. Kibangwar Jamir (b.1938)

Popularly known as Kibangwar retired from the active govt. service in 1999 as Superintending Engineer after a tireless service of 36 and half years. During his service days, he did not dream of making the last Home at Dimapur but when the socio-political unrest was seen too much at his home town, he decided to settle at Dimapur as his second choice. The other reason was the water system makes him annoyed for old aged days. As such he constructed his residential place only after his retirement. The following prospect and problems he is undergoing today.

(a) He has many involvement by being at Dimapur. At 68 he is able to involve in the following organizations; Patkai College. Board as Treasurer, ANCHOR Society a Youth Welfare group, CMHS Board Member, Culture Committee-ODU as member etc. etc. These opportunities may not be there in other towns.

(b) He maintains his private farm in suburb of Dimapur. The accessibility of distance and good communication allows him to enjoy and do something he can in the farm. Plantation of trees and fishery are source of joy at this age.

(c) The other engagements that makes him busy is, he act as the Treasurer for his own Villagers at Dimapur. (Hence, in all social matters and Fellowship works he is involved and could help all his villagers and also who comes from the village are often his guests.

(d) On the topic of Aged Home he feels that, every Nagas are proud to show/tell the society that she/he can take care the aged parents. Sending parents to Aged Home when there are children or relatives is a taboo. The other social factor is Nagas are self-dependant no matter how poor they are. In other words, they are independent loving people rather than depend on someone. He opines that even for ten years from now, the Aged Home may not have any relevance for the Naga Society.

5. Rev. Takomeren (b.1934)

One of the most active old citizens at Dimapur. He started his service as Pastor in Mangmetong Village in 1962 and after serving in various capacities and churches he took retirement in 1999 from Aoyimkum Village Pastor. He was educated at Jorhat and later did his higher studies from Yeotmal.

(a) His purpose of settling in Dimapur was to open a Working Women Hostel. Sharing into deeper feelings of why a working women hostel, he narrates that; during his 44 active years in ministry he has personally did counseled to over 2000 people with different crisis situation. One of the problems he discovered was; most Naga women due to economic or social permissiveness stays with relatives or in-laws house for helping them, studies or also works. But those shelter were not a happy moments for many. They were being harassed, molested to the extend of losing their virginity. As a result of these traumatized situation and feelings many of them became victims of free society and finally remain a problem to the families. He has come to rescue by opening a Home for them. Yet till today, he is unable to fulfil his dreams.

(b) On opinions of running an Aged Home in the social context of the Naga society, he supports that, it has become a necessity with the following reasons; *Firstly,* by opening that house, many aged people can come together and have fellowship, where there will be no sense of boring or lonesome. *Secondly,* helping by the children on monthly basis does not sound very pleasant, but if the helps are through an agency such as a Home, it's become more dynamic rather than an obligation. *Thirdly,* economically, it will be more viable than looking after in their private house. It will also reduce the medical expenses, as the group will be care in one go. *Fourthly,* such Homes will allow them to meet time and again, making their ideas more concrete if any and lastly added to their longevity.

(c) One of the advantages of Dimapur is, its easy communication systems, the modern facilities from transportation to mass media and its accessibility. Some of the examples are, Newspapers are available in the doorstep by early morning, TV/Cable networks are much better, electricity and telephone systems are more advance here. Because, age does not limits the wants of human beings. Aged people need all the things that are wanted by the young!

(d) The disadvantages in the Dimapur can be 'all the busy people are in Dimapur' People are unlimited busy making them to meet more difficult, one should not start without any telephonic appointment.

The Problems and Prospects

Every society has its own dogma. These dogmas bind the society in one way or other no matter how modern they are. Even in the post-modern today without those practices we will be no longer a distinct race. Nagas are no different. With those underlying fabric we can see the pros and cons of the aged in our context. According to Y. Temsu, President Dimapur District Pensioner's Association the importance of Dimapur felt from 1970s and since then it's becoming more and more important. As of now, the land value in city center is Rs.100-150, and suburb is Rs. 35-40 while in outskirts it's Rs.25-30 per sqr. feet. Yet on average everyday ten people are buying a new site for their final settlement. This indicates that more and more people are coming to stay at Dimapur. Among new comers over fifty per cent are retired personnel, thus its becoming the heap of the aged.

As indicated by one of interviewers, there is a great importance for a Recreational Hall for the Aged. When the writer asked what the Pensioner Association are doing among themselves, they have mentioned, about their meeting once in every three months, this is exclusively among the Ao-Nagas. On similar ways, we need to care, provide place for interactions and fellowship.

Today in India Elderly people is increasing at a faster rate than the general population. This is because of the increase in life expectancy rates and decline in the birth rate as a result of improved health care and services. However, with the growth of numbers, the quality of life has gone down. Industrialization, migration, urbanization and westernization have severely affected the value system. Although there was no joint family system within the Nagas, there is a strong family ties than people in many societies, yet the traditional love and care are slowly crumbling down. The changing pace of life has added woes of the older people. What is important to the government is, care for the aged should come as priority and to adopt new measure as an Age pension and working pension. Over 70 per cent of the old population does not get any pension, while people who worked in corporate sector for 30 - 40 years does not get any pension. As per 2004 statistics the Social Security and Welfare provide Rs.100 to 8882 number of old people only. *(Statistical Hand Book of Nagaland 2004: 385).*

Old Age Home: A paradox

Many Nagas opines that, the identity of the Nagas is slowly vanishing. Yet one may agree that, their values, practices, language and customs are to preserve. With this in mind, caring for the aged is a culture for the Nagas. Yet with the growth of 'busy cultures' many children may not have time to stay with the old parents. Thus during the interviewed, many agreed that, if anybody runs a Home for the aged they are willing to come and stay there. Simultaneously, the equal number of people raised their fear that, if such a Home is opened the inmates will be mostly non-Nagas in Dimapur context. While they wish for a place to be together with same age group, an air of hesitation occupies their mind.

There are various confessional provisions for the aged such as in Air or railways. However those privileges can be availed only when one travels out of state. Considering into our parameters the government and society can show a respect; such as travel concession in Nagaland State Transport bus services that are playing within the whole state. On the other hand, today there are many taxes/membership fees to be paid, can there be any relaxation for the Senior friends?

Coping with an Ageing

According to the statistics there are 77 million senior citizens in India and the number is expected to go up to 150 million in the next 25 years. (*www.hinduonnet.com*). The aged from Nagaland will be proud to be added in such multitude number. The growth reasons may thank to medical advances and improvement of nutritious food that led to longer life expectancy. The duty for the government, NGOs and Church are how to help this age group in coping their ageing. One of the reasons why life among the aged happy was (interviewers), their involvement in a New

World and become productive again. Such may require correcting a frame of mind.

From Biblical perspectives we can find many examples those who became productive and achievers. Josh. 14: 6 ff... tells us that, when Caleb boasted of his strength and demanded a new formidable territory he was 85. Moses was no different. When he took the leadership to liberate the Israelites from Egyptian bondage he was 80 (Exo.3: 1 ff). In advance years they may physically weak but they can still use their experiences in one way or other. Dr. Paulson Pulikottil stated 'when physical strength limits the older people to engage in productive labor there are other avenues where they can continue to be used... they had amassed a great wealth of knowledge through experience and contemplation on daily life which could be used for the service of the society' *(Drishtikone* Aug.Nov 2005: 11).

The Naga society can be rightly called as "gerontocracy," especially in the recent past most of the Village elders were old people. They were active, good leaders and consultants. Among the Israelites, the old people were considered to have accumulated a wealth of wisdom and experiences over the years and thus gain a position of respect and authority. Hence old age can be used as a time to shift into a new job. In Dimapur, some of them re-employed as Administrator in various Institutions, and they could earned respect and honor while for the establishment its substantially reduce the overhead cost, as they are working not for salary but rather as service.

For some ageing may be a threat but for those who are willing there are vast areas of scope to learn and enjoy. People those who are attaining 60s and above may expedience the past world 'the world was young'. Today it has many opportunities. With the coming of Computer there are many avenues in IT world making oneself as young learners and enjoys life again. But many could not see these technologies. In Prov.16: 31 we read 'long life is the reward of the righteous; gray hair is a glorious crown'.

Conclusion

Old age is certainly a period that everybody moving for, but all may not like to be called as old. With the change of time to avoid 'aged' we called them as 'Senior citizens' this has come in part as a response to the protest to our elders to the stigma attached to growing old. But whatever name it may be they are worthy to be dignified and honour as found in the ancient cultures. In other words retirement does not connote the subtle message that they have little contribution to the society. With ail dignity they should be treated as special in the society. R.C. Sproul wrote, 'the aged are the valiant ones who have gone too many times to the house of mourning, who have read too many obituaries in the paper, who have survived the rebellions of their children ...They know things we only guess about and exhibit a kindly patience towards our arrogance. ... the onslaught or senility or the embarrassment of incontinence cannot diminish the regal dignity of their person. To them belongs honor. It is their shared right to receive it, and our solemn duty to bestow it. They are the strength and continuity of the family, the patriarchal and matriarchal root of our own dignity'. (1983: 142).

Salute to the Elderly Persons

REFERENCES

Drishtikone. Aug. Nov 2005, Quarterly Magazine of EFICOR. N. Delhi.

Gilmore, John (1992), *Too Young to be Old,* Illinois: Harold Shaw Publishers.

Sproul, R. C. (1983). *In Search of Dignity,* California: Regal Books

Statistical Handbook of Nagaland 2004(2005) Govt. of Nagaland, Kohima

Interviewed:

Ao, Temjen Rev. on August 4, 2006

Er. Jamir, Kibangwar on August 8, 2006

Imti, N. NCS on August 8, 2006.

Rongsenmeren on August 4, 2006.

Temsu, Y Ao on August 11, 2006.

Takomeren, Rev. on August 7, 2006.

8

DIABETES MELLITUS: PROBLEMS AND REMEDIES

—Pardeshi Lal

Diabetes mellitus is a pathological state associated with excretion of sugar in the urine *(glycosuria).* Thus, a diabetic individual continues producing *'honeyed urine'* or urine that is *'sweet at taste'.* The degree of sweetness depends upon the severity of the disease and the amount of sugar discharged in the urine.

It is noteworthy that formation of urine occurs during filtration of blood by the paired kidneys. During the process, blood is filtered by the kidney tubules called *'Nephrones or uriniferous tubules'* where but for proteins and blood corpuscles that are dialyzed, glucose and salts in the blood are filtered. But, as the filtrate advances down the *nephrones,* glucose and majority of salts and water are reabsorbed into the blood capillaries surrounding *nephrones.* This way, fasting blood glucose level is maintained maximum at *110 mg/100ml* of blood. In such individuals, urine is free from glucose. Under any circumstance, if fasting blood glucose levels surpass *140 mg/100ml* of blood, chances of absolute reabsorption of glucose across *nephrones* decrease and individuals become prone to discharge glucose in the urine. Thus, diabetic individuals have sustained high levels of blood glucose (> *140 mg at fast and* > *160 mg postprandial i.e. 2 hours after feeding 75g of glucose in 300ml of water).* The state is described as *chronic hyperglycemia*—the key state that paves the way for manifestation of *diabetes mellitus.*

Diabetes does not spare any age group. However, adults *(after* 35 *years of age)* and *aged people* fall maximum victim to this ailment. The disease has been classified as *Insulin dependent diabetes mellitus (IDDM or Type I diabetes)* and *Non-Insulin dependent diabetes mellitus (NIDDM or Type II diabetes).*

- *IIDM* cases have deficient production of endogenous insulin. Insulin is a polypetide hormone which is naturally synthesized and secreted by β-*cells* of islet of Langerhans of the Pancreas (Figs.1 & 2). Deficient output of insulin may result due to destruction of β-*cell* population caused by mechanical injury, development of benign tumors, or by viral infections - *Mumps and Rubella viruses* - followed by development of autoimmunity to β-*cell* wall. In the past this was also referred as *'juvenile diabetes'* since the disease may manifest even in very young children.
- *NIDDM* manifests usually in middle-age group people and usually persists life-long, hence it is also referred as *'maturity onset diabetes mellitus'.* *NIDDM* normally has a genetic basis, but obese individuals may easily fall victim to this dreaded form of ailment.

A common man unaware of the disease may guess at the onset of *diabetes mellitus* by looking at one or a combination of following features:

- Any wound that does not heal easily.
- Excessive sweating and nervousness associated with loss of memory and eye sight.

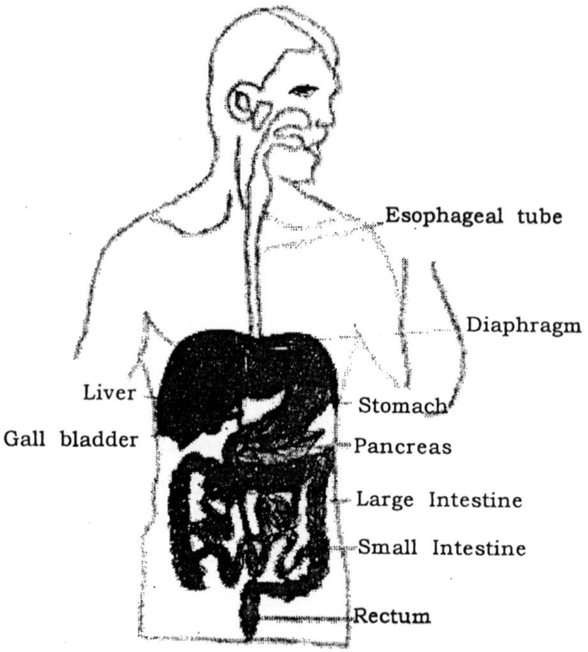

Fig. 1: Diagrammatic sketch showing position of the Pancreas in the human body.

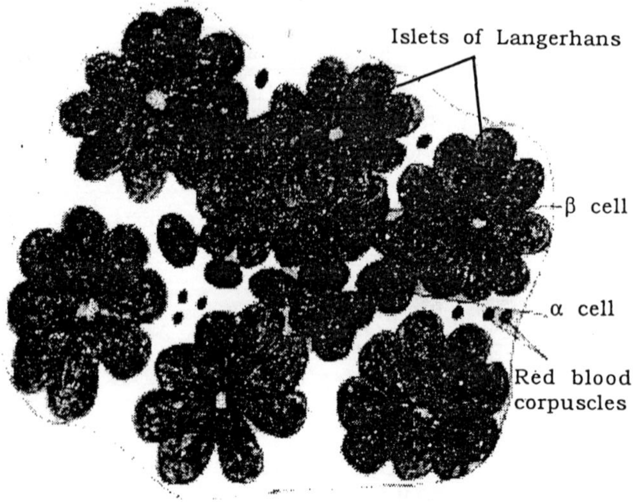

Fig. 2: Transverse section of the Pancreas showing the position of α and β cells that produce glucagons and the Insulin respectively.

- If ants gather to lick the urine passed by a person, it may denote the presence of sugar in the urine.
- Frequent passing of urine *(polyurea or diuresis)* specially after a meal which lasts for few hours.
- Frequent urination is associated with stimulation of thirst and excessive drinking of water *(polydipsia).*
- Excessive stimulation of hunger *(polyphagia),* eating of more food but consistently loosing weight.
- Depletion of muscles in the buttocks, thigh and upper arms *(muscle wasting)* associated with excessive weakness.

It is noteworthy that in an individual all the above features may or may not necessarily manifest together, but it is definite that diabetes mellitus is always associated with high blood glucose levels (hyperglycemia).

Individuals suffering from *glycosuria, polydipsia, polyphagia, and/or muscle wasting* should subject themselves for diagnostic tests as recommended by *World Health Organization,* to ascertain whether they are already falling victim to *diabetes mellitus* or are landing in a safe zone. The tests are based on monitoring blood sugar levels at fast and two hours after meal or feeding 75g of glucose in 300 ml of water. Interpretations are based on blood glucose levels as featured below:

- If fasting glucose levels are between *70-110 mg/ 100 ml* and postprandial (2 hours after feeding 75 g glucose in 300 ml water) levels, *140 mg/ 100 ml* of blood, the person is certainly not diabetic.

- ❖ If fasting blood glucose levels are between *111-140 mg/100 ml* of blood and postprandial levels between 141-199 mg/100 ml, the person is at risk and has impaired *glucose tolerance* level.

- ❖ If fasting glucose levels exceed *140 mg/100 ml* of blood and postprandial glucose levels exceed *200 mg/100 ml,* the person is certainly diabetic.

From the foregoing description, it is clear that *diabetes mellitus* manifests under two conditions:

(i) When patients are deficient in endogenous production of insulin *'insulin dependent diabetes mellitus or IDDM'* and

(ii) The patients are not deficient in endogenous production of insulin, instead circulating levels of insulin are more than normal *'Non-insulin dependent diabetes mellitus or NIDDM'*. But, the common feature in either of the states is that patients have high blood glucose levels or *'hyperglycemia'*.

Insulin is instrumental in facilitating transport of *Glucose, Amino acids, and Free fatty acids* obtained from digested food stuffs, to their target organs like *Liver, Muscles and Adipose tissues.* Simultaneously, it also stimulates all the key enzymes necessary for biosynthesis of *Glycogen, Proteins, and Fats (Lipids)* and their deposition into target tissues. By the same token insulin depresses the activity of all the key enzymes that deplete organ and tissue reserves of these organic compounds.

It may be emphasized that major chunk of food that we eat is comprised of *carbohydrates* which are hydrolyzed into simple sugars such as *glucose and fructose* during the process of digestion. From the intestine, these simple sugars find their way into the blood stream and that is how blood sugar levels increase following a meal or after eating sweets. Once in the blood, some of these sugars are utilized as substrates for metabolic energy, some are retained in the blood *(maximum 120 mg/100 ml)* and the rest is transported to the *Liver and Muscle* for their conversion into *glycogen* and deposition as emergency energy reserves. The transport of sugars across Liver tissues and Muscle cells is normally not permitted and therefore, insulin is required to facilitate the transport of sugars across cell membranes of these tissues. Insulin can accomplish this task on many accounts: (i) Insulin induces orientation and fitting of *GLUT* molecules normally floating in cytosol, into the plasma membrane of Liver and Muscle cells and thus establishes a protein channel for facilitation of glucose movements from blood to these tissues. (ii) In the Liver and Muscle cells, insulin activates all the necessary key enzymes for *phosphorylation* of glucose and fructose and their conversion into glycogen. (iii) Excess of glycogen is diverted towards biosynthesis of fat and its deposition into adipose tissues. Insulin is involved in activating the *lipogenic enzymes.* In the absence of insulin, therefore, glucose entry into Liver and Muscle cells suffers a jolt resulting into glucose retention in the blood. Obviously, sustained levels of glucose in the blood causes hyperglycemia. Excessive amounts of sugars while passing through the kidneys also pose osmotic problems to the kidneys and kidneys may stoop to retain water leading to nephropathy. As such, physiological mechanisms tend to maintain normal circulating levels of sugar and in the process facilitate elimination of excess sugar in the urine. Elimination of glucose in the urine creates a drag for water and that is why diabetics pass more frequent urine compared to normal individuals. Thus, loss of excess sugar in the urine temporarily maintains normal blood glucose levels. It is to be emphasized that brain cells use glucose as an immediate source of metabolic substrate and they continue harvesting glucose from the blood resulting in a concomitant fall in the blood glucose level in due course of time. This obviously stimulates hunger as a demand to maintain blood glucose levels within normal limits primarily to facilitate brains to continue harvesting glucose from the blood to meet its metabolic demands. Once the food is eaten, more than normal levels of glucose become available in the blood and this repeats the forgoing story pending availability of normal levels of insulin.

Lack of insulin severely hampers transport of *Amino Acids* derived from the protein eaten in the food and these find their fate in conversion into glucose *(gluconeogenesis)* aimed primarily, at making blood glucose levels within normal range to facilitate brain cells in harvesting glucose for their metabolic use. In extreme cases, this even leads to Muscle wasting and a depletion of Muscle reserves of the body.

Deficient insulin levels facilitate *lipolytic enzymes* in adipose tissues to produce *Free Fatty Acids* as a metabolic source of energy. The complications arising due to this process are described below under the heading *'Diabetic Keto Acidosis.'*

Non-insulin dependent diabetes mellitus (NIDDM) or adults onset diabetes features a complexity of cellular events that may fall into one of the following categories:

1. The circulating levels of insulin rise in individuals who have insulin resistance and pancreatic islets function normally. Some patients treated with exogenous insulin develop antibodies against the hormone and these proteins inhibit access of the active hormones to its receptors. Insulin resistance may also develop in individuals who produce an abnormal hormone that decreases receptor affinity. Some patients produce abnormal insulin due to

autosomal gene mutation. and/or incomplete cleavage of insulin precursors and a failure to bind with insulin receptors.

2. This may occur due to a decrease in the receptor number and/or their affinity to bind the hormone. Like hormone itself genes forming hormone receptors may have point mutation and receptor malformation. Such receptors while fail to bind insulin, may even be denied access to bind to the plasma membranes. Further, the *b-subunit* of insulin receptors are linked with *tyrosine kinase,* and in certain instances expression of receptor *tyrosine kinase* activity is substantially impaired leading to impaired receptor response to insulin. Yet another form of receptor resistance exhibits formation of antibodies against some portion of the insulin receptors and this some times severely impairs the number and affinity of receptors to respond to insulin.

3. In some cases, gene mutation, leads to insufficient formation of glucose transport molecules and therefore, even though endogenous production of insulin and its receptors are within normal bound, hyperglycemia and diabetes manifest due to failure of transport of glucose across Liver and Muscle cells. In another type of post receptor resistance, fault lies with biosynthesis of hepatic enzyme, *glucokinase,* that *phophorylates* glucose to feed it to glycogenic pathway. Mutation in *glucokinase gene,* thus hampers glucose clearance and results hyperglycemia. This incident may occur even in young individuals and may be 'responsible for a *young onset- type II diabetes.*

Long-term diabetes mellitus, if not treated, may lead to following complications:

1. **Atherosclerosis**—It is a pathological manifestation in which big blood vessels may be partially blocked owing to deposition of lipids in subintimal layers of blood vessels. Although, this complication is very common in non-diabetic obese individuals the disease is particularly common in the diabetics. The physiological bases that account for *atherosclerosis* may be due to following reasons.

   (i) In diabetics, for various reasons, serum cholesterol and *LDL (low density lipid)* tend to be very high and this increases proneness to develop *atherosclerosis.*

   (ii) *LDL* molecules carry most of the *cholesterol* in plasma and in diabetic individuals, they are oxidized and *gycosylated.* Such molecules are deposited in subintimal layers of big vessels causing a*therosclerosis,* As a result of *atherosclerosis,* diabetics are particularly prone to *angina pectoris/ myocardial infarction/ cerebro-vascular accidents etc. It* is noteworthy that diabetics with high blood pressure become more prone to all these complications. Mentally depressed diabetic individuals, are particularly susceptible to *coronary heart diseases* in which arteries supplying to heart muscles get clogged and limit blood supply beyond that point. This may lead to *anoxia* to the affected heart muscles and is characterized by pain in heart (angina) followed by cardiac arrhythmia and heart attack.

2. **Microangiopathy**—This condition is characterized by thickening of capillary-wall leading to obliteration or blood flow through affected capillaries. It is not yet very clear as to what causes the thickening of blood capillaries. One

thing, that seems promising is that prolonged hyperglycemia leads to formation of *sorbitol (an oxidized product of glucose)* in the blood and *sorbitol* in some way causes thickening of blood capillaries. When renal arterial capillaries are involved, it is called *'diabetic retinopathy'* [*also called Kimmelsteil-Wilson Syndrome, (KWS)*] and when renal vessels are affected, it is called as *diabetic nephropathy.*

3. **AGE**: In long standing hyperglycemia, glucose molecules are conjugated with various proteins *(e.g. Hemoglobin or plasma albumin).* Such conjugation occurs either by *'glycosylation'* or by *'glycation'. Advanced glycosylated/glycated end* (AGE) *products* facilitate *atherosclerosis.* In diabetic mellitus, thus, it is a sound policy to estimate *glycosylated hemoglobin or glycosylated plasma albumin* to assess the damage done by the disease.

4. Persistent diabetes may lead to degeneration of *sympathetic/parasympathetic or somatic* or both varieties of nerves can be damaged. Pathological state may manifest into *impotency/ incontinence/ constipation* or loss of *tendon reflexes* (weakness of skeletal muscles *etc.*). Fortunately, brain is not affected.

5. Lack of insulin leads to unsatisfactory combustion of glucose. Therefore, in order to meet the metabolic requirements alternate source of energy as fuel is desired. This necessitates excessive *lipolysis* in the adipose tissues. As a result, massive amounts of *free fatty acids (FFA)* become available. *FFAs* are oxidized in the Liver and produce excessive amounts of *Acetyl Co-enzyme A* (*Acetyl Co. A*). The body mechanisms fail to handle massive production of *Acetyl Co. A* and under such a circumstance, *Acetyl Co. A*

molecules conjugate to form *Aceto-acetic acid*, β-*hydroxy butyric acid* and *acetone*. These are potent metabolites for energy production and are known as *ketone bodies*. *Ketone bodies* are normally excreted in the urine along with *Sodium (Na)* and thus aggravate dehydration. Production of large amounts of *ketone bodies* lead to blood acidosis and failure of buffering mechanisms of plasma. Under such a state, diabetics produce *fruity smell* due to evaporation of *Acetone* through the lungs. Central nervous system is very sensitive to *ketone bodies* and therefore excessive accumulation of *ketone bodies* in the plasma may result paraphylectic, shock, coma and death.

6. Absence of insulin or a lack of response to the insulin results breakdown of muscles. Amino acids thus produced are used for glucose production *(gluconeogenesis)* through the process of *deamination* and *transamination*. The protein stores are thus depleted resulting into *negative Nitrogen balance* and a decrease in body weight. This state is always associated with poor resistance to infections.

   - It is always desired to follow the policy of *"Precaution is better than cure"*. While pursuing with this policy, it is to remember that with ageing metabolic activities decrease and the efficiency of the Metabolic mechanisms in tackling carbohydrates decreases. Obviously, care needs to be taken with respect to eating sweets, starches (Rice, Potato), Oily preparations and the Fatty diets, instead, it is preferred to switchover to Protein-rich diet. This when combined with brisk walk, certainly helps in coping up with Diabetes Mellitus.

- It may be realized that a major chunk of postprandial increase in blood glucose in diabetic individuals is flushed out in the urine on one hand and continuous harvest of glucose by the brain cells from the blood, on the other, makes blood glucose levels fall below the optimum level very soon and this stimulates hunger and eating. If meal is not had then proteins may be mobilized to form glucose. *The diabetics may therefore, afford to skip the medicine but not the meal.* Furthermore, eating too much at one go must be avoided and the same may be adjusted into more than one meal but only after a gap for not less than 4 hours. This would help in avoiding excretion of sugar in the urine and at the same time, would also be able to meet metabolic demands of the brain cells toward glucose.

- Despite taking every possible precaution if diabetes manifests, one should get the blood glucose levels measured and then consult a medical doctor for prescription of the desired medicine. It is a normal practice to go for lowest possible dose of insulin therapy that are commercially available in form of tablets and/ or injections. The sole idea is focused at the minimum dose requirement to keep blood glucose levels within optimum limit. The medicine is taken few minutes before taking a meal.

- Insulin therapy shall however, cope up with diabetes mellitus only in the cases where problem lies due to diminished endogenous production of insulin or when insulin produced by β-*cells* is inadequate and malformed. This would be of no help to the patients having problems associated with malformed insulin receptors or when the etiology of the problems ramifies on a fault with post receptor signal transduction mechanisms. Such patients are advised to pull on with strict dietary regulations as advised by the medical practitioner. Treatments with oral hypoglycemic drugs like *Sulfonureas* and *Metformin* may also help in establizing circulatory levels of glucose in such patients. *Extreme care needs to be exercised while taking exogenous insulin as overdosing of the hormone may result hypoglycemia which may manifest into coma and death.*

9

ACTIVE AGING

—Dr. P. Medem

Aging is a reality of life, and its a continuous process from birth to death. Every tick of the clock, every sunrise of a new day and celebration of every birthday reminds us the process of this phenomenon. Most people are scared, indeed terrified of old age, because they feel that aging is characterized by progressive loss of essential body functions that they have taken it for granted over the years, for instance; loss of vision, diminished hearing, falling of teeth, loss of memory, sexual drive muscle strength and mobility. However, it needs to emphasize that one can become old healthily; means- old age does not necessarily to be progressive deterioration health or susceptibility to a plethora of ailments.

A person from sixty years and above may be generally referred to as old man/woman. The term 'old man' is so distasteful that the new nomenclature generally use is as senior citizen in the lieu of the old people.

The actual factor responsible to live up to a ripe old age entails possessing the right genes. In other words, if your parents and grandparent have led long lives you are like to do so by way of possessing their genes. However, to acquire the right genes are beyond our scope, nevertheless one can increase the chances of growing old healthily. As a matter of fact aging does not take place all of a sudden, and if acquire the proper knowledge and taken remedial measures right from the middle age itself, one can enjoy good physical and mental health complimented with social health.

Contrary to the advertised claims, there is no fountain of youth or magic potion that can prevent the process of aging even the fundamental key question of the subject. Why do we grow old? Still remains unanswered. According to the most accepted theory, progressive free radicals (chemical by product of body) damages cells, tissues and organs, and as our age advances, the body's ability to repair such damages wanes of.

While orientate oneself with the vast field of geriatric care, some fundamental facts are being attempted to unfold in order to keep abreast with this perplexing issue.

Physical fitness is the keyword to lead a satisfying and active life through one's twilight years. Invariably, physical fitness has invaluable ascendancy to a good social life and economic independence which goes hand in hand.

Diet and Nutrition

Diet and nutrition is one factor that will have definite bearing in the process of aging and is most emphasize topic one factor among them all. Medical experts like J. Williams, R.A. Kenny, H.L. Dhar and may others agree that the diet of old people should be continuation of that they consumed in adult life but is less quantity supplemented with vitamins and minerals. As one gets old, the sluggish body movement result to loss of muscle mass and inversely increases fatty tissue requiring less intake of food (carbohydrates and protein). It is agreed that overall intake should be reduced by 15% from age of 45 to 55 years (one decade) thereafter reduction of 10% for each decade. It is accepted fact that by following a 'Balanced Diet' regimen prevent or reduce the most of old age ailments like hypertension, heart disease and diabetes.

In this context, it is useful to bear in mind that antioxidants are natural substances that counter acts the harmful free radicals which damages our body cells. Some recent studies have indicated that antioxidants may help prevent heart disease, some cancer, cataract and other ailments that are common among older people. Among antioxidants that are derived from our food are vitamins A, C, and E which is why most experts recommended five servings of fruits and vegetables a day. The contemporary health care system emphasize more on the preventive aspect than on curative, consequently, antioxidants have gained much importance in modern medicine. Many drugs companies are manufacturing antioxidants under different brands which are now readily available over the counter. However, it is noteworthy that fruits and vegetables are best source of antioxidants and the synthetic antioxidants are for those who cannot manage to get daily rations of fruits and vegetables.

In a recent study conducted by J.C. Patel have indicated that decrease of overall risk of various diseases in those who follow vegetarian diet. Moreover, apart from the increased immunity against various diseases, it may be also contributory in delaying aging process. As per popular saying 'you are what you eat' there is not alternative to eat healthy food. Let us eat healthy food and live healthy life.

Environment and Personal Hygiene

Elderly people are more susceptible to infections, and maximum death occurs as a results of respiratory tract inflection particularly *bronchopneumonia.* In old aged people the respiratory tract secretion become more copious and failure to clear it in time and completely, invites organism to flourish in the secretion giving raise to *bronchopneumonia* resulting to infection. Infection may also prop up from the unhygienic surrounding, filthy clothing poor personal hygiene. Improper diet and also frequently compromising to eat leftover cool food may lead to stomach upset. Such interrelated unfavorable conditions such as poor economic status, general weakness and restricted mobility and poor vision which often associated with old aged people are found to be root-cause. Most of old people face a lot of difficulty in taking care of daily own needs which require to be addressed. Good personal hygiene and maintaining clean surrounding is the mainstay to keep away from constant source of infection.

Exercise

Staying active is a terrific way to stave off the negative effects of old age, because it helps your body to maintain, improves and even repairs itself. Involving in physical activities improves joint flexibility, improves muscle strength, lowers blood pressure and strengthens bones by way of preventing *osteoporosis*. It also promotes lungs functions thereby preventing *bronchial asthma* which is the single most killer of old aged people. Sweat centre is depressed in elderly subject and sweating not an indication of adequate exercise in elderly. Brisk walking for a period of 45 minutes to one hour is most ideal exercise for elderly subjects. Early morning hours when the traffic is minimal considered to be the most ideal time to undertake walking exercise. Remember to start out slowly, exercising about 5-10 minutes twice a week, gradually build up to a higher level of activity. Choose an activity that you will enjoy, and try to get a friend to accompany and encourage you in time of laziness. Swimming, gym exercise and yoga are few other options best suited for aged people. Before starting your exercise regimen, remember to check with your doctor about suitability, complications or risks of the particular exercise you have chosen.

Periodical Health Check-up

Old aged people usually suffer from multiple pathologies even though some of them may not know the existence of their ailment. For instance, community survey in Great Britain by L.C. Hamdy *et al.* has shown that 14% of the otherwise normal elderly subjects suffer from border line congestive cardiac failure and hypertension.

As one grow old, the body undergoes a lot of changes which may be indicated by decline in appetite, with loss lack of speech and memory loss. These symptoms may be due to normal process of old age or sometime they may be due to diseases such TB, Diabetes and Cancer which calls for periodical check up for proper screening. If such diseases are identified in an early stage is possible to provide suitable treatment with better patient outcome.

Sex, Aging and Health

Contrary to popular opinion, most senior citizens want to enjoy active and satisfying sexual lives. The natural process of aging and physical changes may sometime adversely affect sexual intimacy and capacity. Contrary to this belief, gerontologist and medical experts agree that sexual interest and activities can be longevity enhancing factor for old man and woman. Sexual activities seem to have protective affect particularly on a man's health. In a cohort study of G.D. Smith *et al.* and J.T. Freeman found that morality risk in man found to be 50% lower in man with high frequency of orgasm. The reason may be that during the sexual activities our body releases a substance called *endorphin* (morphine like substance) produce in our brain which rejuvenates our body cells.

No doubt sexual desire diminishes as the age advances but many remains sexually active even other the age of eighty which should not be suppressed. However, biologically woman's sexuality is less affected than men.

Aging, Loneliness and Solitude

Loneliness is a deadly enemy of old age people. Research has shown that senility sets in six times faster in a person who is isolated and withdrawn from the society. They tend to become more and more isolated leading to depression resulting in increased tendency to commit suicide.

Inversely, solitude is beneficial. In solitude one is able to turn to the spiritual side in the company of the spiritual inner being, thus one never feels lonely.

Mental and Social Well-being

A sound mind can exist only in a sound body. However, mental health is also dependent on social harmony family relation and independent financial status.

The degeneration of brain cells during old age can be avoided or reduced by actively involving either in creating work or recreation such as reading book, listening to radio, mixing with friends and relatives. One can learn new hobbies like painting, writing books, becoming computer literate etc. The idea behind is, to keep the brain cells busy and activating to avoid or reduce from degeneration.

Socially, one may contribute by volunteering for social work, teaching in institutions, taking part in religious activity to keep them busy. It is found to be beneficial that elders of a community may from a club and meet together periodically. In such meetings they can choose to discuss on any topic from folk-lore to contemporary burning issues. Some of them may be entrusted to follow up popular TV serials and analyze beneficial and ill affects of such serial in our society. Active involvement in community works and learning to live together with the masses is also considered as one of the best social medicines for old age which is known as active theory.

The twilight years can become a bank of wisdom for younger generation if utilize their experience wisely instead of becoming extra burden to our family and society.

Financial Status

A comfortable or independent financial statu contributes largely to mental satisfaction and als enables timely physical care. Many of the elderly peopl have financial difficulties which often start durin period of retirement leading to worriness. One may no worry consciously, but sub-consciously these thoug undermines his sense of confidence.

Hence, right from the middle age when one i physically active and financially sustainable, on should take adequate planning to ensure a comfortabl financial position in old age. They also should mak it a point to retain their property and wealth in the own name until death. And also should have regula saving accounts in a bank nearby them.

Conclusion

Most of the old people face a lot of difficulties in taking care of their own needs due to the persisten health problem such as diminished hearing, failing vision, loss of memory and restricted mobility and above that it may be supplemented by financial problem. Many of them may loss control over their bodily function. Some become even disabled and remain confined to a wheelchair or bed as a result, home for aged age becoming increasingly popular in India so that older people live together in support each other when their own families are no longer willing to do so.

The twilight years are likely to lead to unfortunate increase in illness supplemented by additional burden of unwelcome medical bills. As the biological system start failing gradually assortment of medical problems may develop. Development of multiple medical problems often entails them subject to multiple medications and perhaps may consult different doctors as well. Certainly older patient have special health care needs. Thus, as the health care pattern become more complex it also becomes more fragmented. Consequently, geriatric health care has attained the status of speciality in many parts of the world. However, India still stands far behind than other developed countries in the field of geriatric care. Until the national geriatric care policy is fully operational, personal and family awareness and care is the mainstay of combating this universal problem.

> *Growing old is a bad habit which a busy man has no time to form.*
>
> *—Andre Maurois*

REFERENCES

Dhar, H.L., Aging gracefully. *Ind J Clin Pract.*, 1999; 10(1): 61-66.

Dhar, H.L., Health and aging. *Ind J Med Sc* 1997: 51 (10): 373-77.

Dhar, H.L., Nutrition and Aging. *Bombay Hos J*, 1997: 39:159-61.

Dhar, H.L., Physiology of aging. *Ind J Med Sc.*, 1997; 52(ii):485-97.

Dhar, H.L., Specific problems of health in elderly. *Ind J Med Sc.*, 1993; 47(12): 285-92.

Hamdy, L.C., Zakaria, G.Y., A special clinic for the over 65 in a GPs surgery. *Practitioner* 1977; 291:365.

Kenney, R.A., Aging process in physiology of aging synopsis. *Year book Medical* publishers Inc., London. 1982; 11-20.

Kraise, M.V., Mohan, L.K. (eds.), *Food Nutrition and Diet Therapy* (3rd ed.) WB. Saunders Company, 1984; 99-180.

Law, R Charlmerse, Medicine and elderly people. A general practice survey. *Brit Med J* 1976; 1:565-68.

Pargaonkar, K.A., and Dhar, H.L., *Evaluation of Exercise Induced Asthma (EIA), Effects of Various Drugs: A Double Blind Cross Over Study.* Excerpta Medical, Oxford 1991; 569-75.

Patel, J.C., Prevention of aging. *Ind. J Med Sc* 1997: 51(10): 364-72.

Raju, P.S., Madhavi, S., Prasad, K.B.V., Comparison if Effects of Yoga and Physical Exercise in Athletes. *Ind J Ved Res* 1994; 100: 81-87.

Singh, R.B., Rastogi, S.S., Ghosh, S., *The Diet and Moderate Exercise trial* (DAME).

Udapa, K.N., *Yoga and Meditation,* Sivanandanagar, UP, India, Divine Life Society. 1975.

William, J., Miline J.S., "Research methods in aging" in: *Textbook of Geriatric Medicine and Gerontology* (2nd ed.), JC Broklehust Churchill Livingstone, New York, 1978.

10

VALEDICTORY SPEECH

—D. Baruah

I am very much grateful to the organizers of this seminar, particularly to Prof. A. Lanunungsang, Program Director, Department of Sociology Nagaland University, Lumami for giving this honor to be the Guest of Honor in this Valedictory session though I do not deserve it.

I hope the participants have learnt many things about the problems of aged in our society and the needs for their care from the valuable papers presented by scholars representing various field of studies. I wish to congratulate them.

There has been a time when the elders were neglected in the society. In some societies according to traditions the parents were left alone uncared when the children got married and separated. But in some societies there were joint families where parents and married children lived together sharing everything together. But in many societies, this culture has also broken.

Time has changed now. Life is changing so fast through science and technology calling computer-age and even the Gandhian philosophy of "simple living and high thinking" life and his valuable ideas on politics, economics, education and social problems have become redundant. Elders have been neglected for some generations.

But now, the elders are happy that the world has awakened to look after their problems. UN Secretary General, Kofi Annan, in the "Second World Assembly on Ageing in Madrid" declared, "We have neglected the elders for many years. From now on, all the countries of the world should think to give proper place to the senior citizens, in the last phase of their life, while making national development plans-social, political and economic."

India has also accepted the proposal of the UNO and now offering several facilities/benefits to the senior citizens through the Ministry of Social Justice and Empowerment to the elders of 65 years above such as:-

1. 30% concession travel by train,
2. 50% concession in domestic air flight,
3. Rebate in income tax,
4. Priority in telephone connection,
5. Priority in the court cases,
6. .05% more interest in fixed deposit in the bank,
7. 10 kgs of rice monthly to those who are not receiving old age pension under Anna Purna Scheme.
8. Separate queue/counter for elders,
9. 90% subsidy to any project for the elders runs by NGOs.

First October is observed as "International Day for the Elderly". Last year, I also have participated in one such seminar for elderly people organized by Women Department of Mokokchung Town Ao Baptist Church, where free medical check-up for the elders was successfully arranged with the help of medical staff of Imkongliba Memorial Hospital, Mokokchung.

Mokokchung District Pensioners' Association has constructed "A Day Care Centre" for the elders. This is also a very good project for elderly people. Programs like this should make a regular activity in a place like this in this newgeneration.

I hope, the outcome of this seminar should be meaningfully implemented by the concerned authorities for the benefit of elderly people.

May God bless this Seminar.

D. Baruah,
Retd. O.S.D. (Edn.)
Mokokchung,

17.08.2006

The Older the Wiser.

RECOMMENDATIONS

—Prof. A. L. Ao

At the end of one day seminar on the theme **Understanding the Problems of Old Aged People and the Need for Care** the following resolutions have been adopted by the participants of most honorable elderly people:

1. Establishment of Old Aged Recreational Home/ Day Care Centre creating at least minimum facilities in every district headquarters in the state of Nagaland.
2. Issuance of Old Aged Certificate to the elderly people by the competent authority for the purpose of availing welfare measures as per the provision extended to the elderly people.
3. Enhancement of Old Aged Pension both by the State Government and Central Government by identifying the deserving elderly people.
4. Timely payment of Service Pension as per Central Service Pension Rules 1972, sub rule 64 to the retired employees/family pension without delay.
5. Opening up of separate queue/counter for elders in the banks/ticket counter in every important place in the state.

6. Creation of facilities by the concerned authorities/department for Free Master Health Check-Up for elderly people.

7. Awareness program on the rights of the aged be generated through school curriculum, religious organizations, NGOs, media and community as a whole.

INDEX